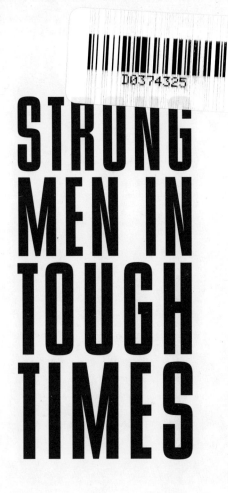

STRUNG MEN IN TOUGH TIMES

STRONG MEN IN TOUGH TIMES

EDWIN LOUIS COLE

watercolor books®
Southlake, Texas

Second Edition

Strong Men in Tough Times
ISBN 978-1-931682-07-7

Copyright © 1993 Estate of Edwin Louis Cole®

Ed Cole® Library
P.O. Box 92921
Southlake, TX 76092

www.EdCole.org

Published by Watercolor Books®
P.O. Box 93234
Southlake, TX 76092

www.watercolorbooks.com

Printed in the United States of America

DEDICATION

To the memory of three strong men:

Ralph Davis, a "man of God," who never met a man he didn't influence for God. From my childhood memories, I can still see his faded blue eyes, brimming with tears as he prayed, hear his voice in loving concern, telling about Jesus, and visualize him, carrying his big black Bible wherever he went.

Ralph Calkins, my "second dad," who loved me even in my wild days and wicked ways, whose patience with this prodigal helped bring me to my senses.

C. E. Britton, a "man among men," whose deformed spinal condition from a childhood injury refused him a painless moment, yet who became one of the world's foremost Bible scholars and expositors; a true "prince of the pulpit," who taught me by example the true greatness of men.

CONTENTS

ONE

THE CHALLENGE

After a recent ministry trip on the East Coast, I boarded a flight for home. The huge airliner gleamed on the tarmac, but inside stood rows of seats better suited for a school bus than adult travelers. I jostled my neighbor as I tried to slide my case below the narrow seats in front of us.

"Can they fit any more seats on this plane?" I joked.

The well-dressed man next to me smiled, and we began to chat. His name was Charles, an executive with a well-known investment firm. When I told him my occupation was writing and speaking to men, his face grew somber and his conversation serious. From his vantage point of global economics, he confided in me his fears of the changing world.

So severe are the difficult times we're entering that he has grave concerns for the welfare of his children. Although a devoted father, he felt a tinge of regret that he brought his children into the world to face what he now considers a dangerous and difficult future. His parental concerns led to changes in his personal life, and he now spends more time training his children educationally and morally. "I feel responsible to help them be prepared for whatever comes," he said.

His statements echoed the growing concerns I have heard from men the world over. In recent years, I've noticed a trend—whether in South Africa, Norway, Germany, New Zealand, Australia, England, Mexico or the Philippines. While each nation has its unique problems, an underlying moral and spiritual decay has led to this common dilemma: Men seem to feel uncomfortably responsible yet out of control.

In all of human history, there has never been a time when the call for strong men was louder or the need greater.

The Dream

All men dream of being lauded as heroes, but few know what it takes or how to get there. God created men to be leaders and heroes. That's why every man dreams of himself in a heroic act: It's the bottom of the ninth in the seventh game of the World Series. Your team is behind with the score five to two. The bases are loaded, you're at bat, and the count is three balls and two strikes. You have only one more pitch to hit, and you zing it over the fence for a grand slam and run the bases into history. Or, your bride is lying on the railroad tracks, tied down by the villain who is slinking away. You ride to her rescue just in the nick of time. Her hero! Or you bring food through the harrowing jungle to rescue the starving children. Of such stuff are heroic fantasies created.

Yet far from living strong, heroic lives, men are scrambling to regain a sense of manhood that seems to have vanished. Through "wildman" gatherings, books, lectures, new philosophies and religions, they are trying to absorb some lost manhood, as if a vapor in a vanishing dream. Some intangible force has emasculated that manhood–that quality that seems now to linger only in history books and biographies. The more men try to grasp it, the more fleeting it seems, and the more frustrated they become.

Men know that some things are more important than life itself. Heroes, martyrs and soldiers give their lives for causes they deem more valuable than themselves.

In the quest for self-fulfillment, self-awareness and self-gratification, masses of men have lost what it means to be a man, a hero, a leader. We have sold morality for economic privilege. We have lost our dignity as producers in the workforce. In frustration, we have succumbed to the stresses of eroded manhood and lost our ideals to immoral, illegal, unethical or irresponsible actions.

The world is crying for strong men who will overcome drifting philosophies and bring order, hope and dignity back to a world in desperate need of men who will be heroes. Immorality, greed, pride and fear of financial calamity have all taken their toll. Statesmanship has been swallowed up by political expediency. Stewardship of major businesses has been devoured by greed. Philanthropic guardianship has been pillaged by pride. Apprenticeship has been scrapped by financial efficiency.

Today's world is progressing technologically but regressing morally and spiritually. Fathers who try to develop their children to be good citizens, obey the laws, exhibit integrity and behave morally are disgusted with the fierceness of the lewd who demand license for lascivious lifestyles. They are fed up with lawless youth who are better armed than standard street cops and with the hate-filled music lyrics that pollute the air to inspire rebellion against constituted government and family. While their outrage burns, today's actively moral men are portrayed as an anachronistic throwback to some Victorian era which has no relevance to modern mores. Parent-bashing is only their newest concern.

No wonder the Proverb says, "The good hate the badness of the wicked. The wicked hate the goodness of the good."[1] Americans have sunk to new lows of lying, cheating and stealing, especially among the young. In the Orient, where a higher standard is held for honesty in schooling, the older generation is concerned about the corruption of their sons and daughters who go to school in the United States, succumb to a lower moral standard and come home to cheat on exams.

Politicians and pundits who call for a higher standard, greater regard for family and good will among men are mocked by the liberal media. They are lightning rods for the vast majority of people who are still trying to hold on to moral values, ethical behavior and honest character in spite of culture's decline.

The Strength

The strength of a man is in his moral fiber.

Strength is always proven by resistance. To prove how strong glue is, place it on two pieces of material, put them together, then try to pull them apart. The strength of a marriage is determined by the ability to resist forces that try to pull the partners apart. The strength of a nation, church or family depends on the character of its members to withstand the pressures to tear it apart. Most defeated nations and families collapse from within, which makes them vulnerable from without.

The same is true with individuals. A man's inner strength determines his ability to withstand temptations, accusations, persecutions, seductions, lies and other pressures that work to enervate. He must have strength to stand against wrong and for right.

The world needs strong men.

God created man and every other living thing and ordered them to produce after their own kind. According to His design, orange trees produce oranges. Oysters produce pearls. Men produce manhood. God doesn't expect men to produce oranges or pearls, angels or perfection. God's only expectation of men is manhood.

One man perfectly exemplified the traits of manhood so elusive to us today. He retained them as He laid down His own life. He accepted responsibility not just for His own actions, but for the actions of the entire world. He taught men that only by losing one's life would one truly gain it. By the example of His life and His teachings, He left us the principles that would always make us heroes.

In the United States, we cannot mention His Name in publicly-supported places, must not laud Him or celebrate His birth or death openly; dare not use His Name in prayer at political gatherings (though politicians rely on His words in their speeches and swear to uphold the laws He established and fulfilled on earth). Though forces have tried to erase Him from society's conscience, yet He continues to teach men how to rise to greatness, to become real men, to achieve the heroic successes we dream of achieving. This man is Jesus Christ.

He is not the Christ of religionists, nor the "great man" of philosophers, but the Christ of God, the embodiment of everything originally created in man, the "image" of God. As God once inscribed His commandments on the tablets of stone for Moses, now, because of the ability of Christ's Spirit to dwell within, He inscribes them on the tablets of men's hearts.[2] Men of God desire to do the will of God, not from external, legal motivation, but because of an inward, spiritual desire created by God Himself. That inward Presence re-creates the spirit of the man and renews his mind.

For men to be men once again, we must regain the spirit of manhood in virility and integrity, the power of manhood in productivity and leadership, the conviction of manhood in resolve and moral excellence.

We are entering a tough time for this world. It is tougher than ever to fulfill our dreams. God said the earth would wear out like a cloth.3 The holes in the earth's atmosphere are indicators of His veracity. Signs of the times, as foretold by prophets of God, portend the difficulties that lie ahead. The world is in transition, Europe is in a furor, Asia is upset, and Africa is threatened by anarchy. Plus, the United States is no longer the Christian nation it once was, but it is becoming a foreign nation to committed Christians. We need to realize it's going to take a strong man to live through these times successfully and achieve his dreams.

For men to be men once again, we must regain the spirit of manhood in virility and integrity, the power of manhood in productivity and leadership, the conviction of manhood in resolve and moral excellence.

As moral absolutes are replaced by situational ethics; right and wrong are erased by what is politically correct; sedition is accepted as the norm for change; truth is turned backward …

As justice is perverted by legalities; lawmakers are more concerned for criminals' rights than for victims and families; genocide is legalized for the unborn, ailing and aged …

As famine is created by tribal warfare; neighborhoods become guarded communities; people return to ancient ages by "walling" themselves in to ward off invaders …

As the degeneration of human philosophy eventuates into a form of solipsism—the "worship of self"—where the only right in life is what pleases self …

As value systems that shaped relationships in the world become introverted and culture itself is lost in coarse selfishness, which, in itself, is the core of sin …

As we find these things occurring, the world becomes an ever-more-dangerous place.

In such a world, fear begins to cause the hearts of men to fail. Fear replaces hope. Reality finds escape in fantasy. Succumbing to the desire to believe a lie is easier than contending for the truth.

In this environment, the voice that promises to quell the riotous and bring stability and peace to the peoples of the nations will not only be heard, it will be yielded to. The vast law-abiding class in nations around the world will be willing to surrender total authority to such a person in exchange for peaceful promises, regardless of his or her moral or spiritual values. The realistic, yet horrible, prognosis, if such a thing happens, is to have a world leader who uses the radical criminal element in concerted alignment to control the very people who voluntarily surrendered their power.

Such an occurrence would not be a first of its kind but could well be the last.

The Model

At a similar time in ancient history, a man who used the godly principles that Christ would embody hundreds of years later became the greatest influence in the world. He held firm to his religious beliefs, faced the grim realities of the age and contended for truth in a world of lies and false images. He was endowed with the attributes that make men great—integrity, moral excellence, character, a God-fearing spirit, political savvy, immeasurable courage, decisiveness and a strong, handsome appearance that emanated from a strong spirit. He lived during persecution, political upheaval and oppression; survived conspiracies against him, false accusations, near-fatal encounters, economic disaster and war. He was a strong man for the tough times in which he lived. Daniel was his name; serving God was his game.

Three women brought Daniel to my attention while I was in Harare, Zimbabwe. As I was traveling through their country, holding meetings, the woman approached Chris, a former police inspector who was helping me. They told him they wanted to explain something to me. Tight scheduling prevented me from meeting them, so he passed on their message to me.

Being a former military officer, Chris first gave me a background briefing on his country. Rhodesia was in armed conflict for roughly fourteen years until it became Zimbabwe. During the war, the men spent six weeks in the bush fighting, then six weeks at home, working before returning to the bush. The tension and anxiety in the homes and nation were tangible.

During the fighting, godly women banded together to pray earnestly for their men and nation. As time went by, people called them "Esthers," named after the queen who saved her nation from destruction. Rhodesian women, praying for their nation, believed they had come to their country for "such a time as this."4

After years of fighting, the war ended abruptly. As their men returned home, the women perceived they had become passive, complacent and lethargic. The "Esthers" saw the need for intercession as much then as during the war. As they prayed for the men, their families and the weight of responsibility they carried, an answer came to them. I believe it is truly a word for men, not only of Zimbabwe, but of this entire generation. It is so simple, yet so profound: *"There was a time for Esthers, but today is a time for Daniels."*

Their words brought the story of Daniel up to date for me. Daniel was a teenager when his country collapsed from sin and moral decay. The conquering king of Babylon, Nebuchadnezzar, chose Daniel to be trained, tutored and fitted for service as an adviser in his foreign court. Daniel's integrity, character and trust in God rallied his captive friends, who advanced with him in esteem and prominence. The predictions and interpretations God gave to Daniel endeared him to the king. He became a statesman, rising to second-in-command under Nebuchadnezzar, and he repeated his performance through three kings and their administrations. As an aged man, he was thrown to the lions, only to be protected by God.

We may never gain the reputation Daniel maintained from his youth, but we can learn the elements that enabled him to surmount every hardship and obstacle and to experience elevation to a position of authority. He survived a crumbling society and relocation to a foreign land and proved himself a valuable asset to three successive kings.

A pastor named Gary Stone wrote me a letter with the following list of Daniel's attributes:

• unashamed boldness	• immeasurable blessing
• uncommon standard	• unlimited influence
• unearthly protection	• unhindered persistence
• unblemished faith	• unusual test

STRONG MEN IN TOUGH TIMES

We don't have Daniel to elect to political office, teach the church or place on the company board of directors, but we do have the spirit of Daniel, the manhood of Daniel, the principles of Daniel and the example of Daniel from which we can learn and develop as men.

Jesus said we are to love God with all our hearts, souls, strength and minds.[5] Job said, "Just as my mouth can taste good food, so my mind tastes truth when I hear it."[6] Men today must acquire a taste for truth if they want to maximize their manhood.

Men without an organized system of thought will always be at the mercy of men who have one. In this present age, we must awaken ourselves to the urgent need to study, restore our love for truth and renew our reverence for God's Word.

The men I am privileged to minister with in various parts of the world have backgrounds ranging from crime to wealth to homosexuality to middle-class blandness–before experiencing God's transforming power. Their lives prove that to become part of God's nobility, one needs no pedigree. God knows no barrier to His grace, no boundaries to His love and no power that can stop the redemptive work of His Spirit in men's lives. God will make any willing male into a real man.

The Call

Yesterday, I was talking with a distraught father whose daughter is marrying a man who rejects Christ. A Christian college graduate, she made her choice because, as she angrily put it, "all single Christian men are wimps." Young men have been influenced by the world and mass-marketing strategists to squander their vitality on sensual lusts and self-gratifying desires. We needn't wonder why they don't withstand the pressures of the changing world.

The call for strong men is not just for married men to bring their lives, families and businesses into order. It's also for single men who are tired of bending to the world's pressures and want to discover and revel in the strength of manhood. The world needs men who know they are men, not wimpish males. We need men who are strong in their manhood, able to rise to any occasion, to shape nations. Anyone who thinks the Bible is outdated is unrealistic. There is nothing more relevant on earth today than the published Word of the Creator God. Whose wisdom can compare to God's?

Men who are not interested in acquiring godly manhood will not make it through the next chapter of this book. It takes more than a casual desire to learn anything. The great baseball pitcher Nolan Ryan excited the world when he pitched his seventh no-hitter. An edited video of his pitches, showing one after another successively, looks like a continuous replay of the same pitch. He never deviated from the habits he learned in practice. His devotion to develop in private what he wanted to perform in public made him great. The same concentration is needed to achieve greatness in any endeavor.

The lowest level of knowledge is assumption. Above that is knowledge, then understanding, then wisdom (which is applied knowledge), then skill and finally practice. One can know and understand something and even do it successfully once or twice, but the ability to accomplish the same thing routinely is where true success is found. The greatest of men discipline themselves to practice.

Heroes are men who act in a moment of time on a need greater than self.

Daniel studied and practiced his manhood and faith in God. He caught the attention of kings who looked up to him, not because he was a great orator, a political success or a palm-pressing man-pleaser, but because of his lifestyle. He was not a leader made by man but a leader made by God.

The man is more than the message. Daniel's life proved this. Daniel's message was credible because he was. When the man is no longer credible, his message is suspect.

The goal of our lives is not to live life to the maximum but to sustain maximized living. To do that, we must be established in our manhood with God as our foundation. Fame can come in a moment, but greatness comes with longevity. Great men are those who sustain their achievements over years, regardless of what the years bring. Men today must prepare to sustain themselves in the uncertain years that lie ahead.

The 1990s have been called a decade of destiny, a decade of decision, a decade of daring, a decade of desperation—but whatever you want to call it, this decade finds the world in transition. As a result, there is incredible spiritual, emotional and mental turbulence going on in men's lives and in families everywhere.

Daniel was prepared when his time came, having dedicated himself to God and developed the character that qualified him for leadership. Daniel became a hero to the Israelites of his day and is a hero of faith to us today.

Heroes are men who act in a moment of time on a need greater than self.

You can be a hero. You can have the spirit of Daniel. You don't have to become a preacher, a missionary or an evangelist to be a real man. God doesn't want to change your personality, your drive or your ego. He wants to sanctify those things when you consecrate them to Him. God expects only one thing from you—manhood.

Read on for a challenge, an exhortation and a simple blueprint for living a heroic, fulfilling life as a man.

End Thoughts

- Some things are more important than life itself.
- Men without an organized system of thought will always be at the mercy of men who have one.
- The man is more than the message. The message is credible because the man is.
- Heroes are men who act in a moment of time on a need greater than self.

Reflections

1. How is today's world different than when you were a child?
2. What set Daniel apart from other men?
3. Do you have a dream that you'd need to become a "Daniel" to attain? What can you do this week in private that would help you pursue that dream?

TWO

THE ULTIMATE DECISION

A friend of mine named Larry Kerychuk, director of an international ministry to athletes, had a grandfather who was similar to Daniel in some ways. Let me explain first what I mean about Daniel.

Daniel was purposed in heart, determined in spirit and resolute that nothing would deter, distract or detour him from serving Jehovah God. Daniel's discipline of daily devotion to God undergirded his decisions. His belief in God served as the foundation for his life.

When unscrupulous and jealous men conspired to undermine Daniel's influence on the king, they watched for a weakness in his life. Unable to discover a flaw, they decided to use his strength as a weakness. They determined to have his practice of openly praying three times each day banned by civil law. By use of fawning flattery, they advised the king that only his god should be worshipped and that anyone found worshipping another god should be punished. They knew from Daniel's lifestyle that he would never capitulate to worship any god other than Jehovah.

When Daniel disobeyed the king's new edict, the result was a night in a den of hungry lions. Daniel refused to bow to a civil edict that was contrary to known righteousness. His civil disobedience wasn't a result of rebellion against the king but of resolve to do God's will, regardless of the consequences. Against an order that was intended to destroy life, Daniel was undeterred. Under the threat of certain death, he prayed. It's common knowledge that the lions' mouths were shut, Daniel was saved and his conspirators were devoured by the lions which they had intended for him. God's ironic vengeance.

Daniel was a man of resolve. He believed in his heart—"purposed in his heart."[1] His heart was united in its resolution. There is power in unity. "Unite my heart to fear thy name" is the prayer of the psalmist.[2] An established, united heart gives great strength of mission.[3]

Larry Kerychuk's grandfather, a man of deep conviction acquired from studying and obeying God's Word, was in the Russian army during World War I. His relationship with Christ was founded on a rich personal experience of spiritual transformation. The wonder of his salvation enraptured his heart with love for Jesus Christ and gave him a burning desire to share the same knowledge with every man he met.

The Russian captain in charge of Larry's grandfather's unit grew increasingly enraged with his overt witnessing of Jesus to the troops. It wasn't enough that the grandfather was talking one-on-one to men, but he was preaching to groups of men and would not heed the command to stop. Finally, out of a hatred that could not restrain itself, the captain tied the grandfather to a tree, placed a cannon in front of him and told him that if he did not promise to stop preaching Christ, he would blow him to pieces.

Facing the cannon, the stalwart, spirited believer said without flinching, "Fire away! I will not stop!"

The captain didn't fire, but he sent Larry's grandfather to prison for four years. When he was released, he emigrated to Canada. There, in the pristine beauty of the cold northlands, he continued to work and preach. Going from village to town, preaching in homes, halls and whatever location was available, he evangelized the fellow immigrants and citizens of his adopted country.

Perseverance will always outlast persecution.

Years went by until, unbeknownst to him, the Russian captain who threatened his life also emigrated to Canada. Once when Larry's grandfather was preaching in a small village while making his circuit of cities and towns, he was within a mile of the captain's new home. A friend of the captain's invited him to attend the meeting. Still adamantly opposed to the Gospel, the captain, as a courtesy, agreed to go with his friend.

The captain entered the crowded room warily and watched as people sang and clapped their hands. Then a man stepped to the front, and the captain was taken aback. When the man began to speak, the captain recognized him as the soldier who would not stop preaching years before. Overwhelmed that their paths would once again cross in such a distant place and ashamed at what had once been, the captain startled the crowd by falling to his knees and weeping. Before long, the two men were embracing one another as brothers in Christ.

Unhindered persistence was the resolve of both Larry's grandfather and Daniel.

Perseverance will always outlast persecution.

The Importance of Believing

The great philosopher, Aristotle, taught that heavy objects fall to the ground faster than light ones. Because he was one of the greatest thinkers of all time, people believed him. Finally, two thousand years after Aristotle's death, Galileo summoned learned professors to the base of the Tower of Pisa. Then he climbed to the top and pushed off a ten-pound weight and a one-pound weight at the same time. Much to everyone's amazement, both landed at the same time. The power of belief in conventional wisdom was so strong, however, that the professors refused to believe what they had seen. They denied Galileo's experiment and insisted Aristotle was right. The strength of their belief in what they had been taught would not allow them to admit they were wrong. Rather than accept the truth, they persisted in believing an inaccurate teaching.

A person's beliefs hold the greatest potential for good or harm in life. What is believed about God holds the potential for death or life everlasting.

Many men are taught wrong and thus believe wrong, and yet they hold to it so strongly that they would rather stay wrong than admit it and change. But there are times when change is vital.

There is an old story about a ship's captain who one night saw what looked like the light of another ship heading toward him. He had the signalman blink to the other ship, "Change your course ten degrees south."

The reply came back, "Change your course ten degrees north."

The ship's captain answered, "I am a captain. Change your course south."

To which the reply was, "I am a seaman first class. Change your course north."

This infuriated the captain, so he signaled back, "I say change your course south. I'm on a battleship!"

The reply came back, "And I say change your course north. I'm in a lighthouse."

Refusal to change can bring disaster.

It's a truism that if someone says something wrong and fifty thousand people repeat it—it's still wrong. Sounds silly, yet people believe falsehoods every day regarding Jesus. They believe in evolution, a theory never proved, yet refuse to believe in proven Christianity.

Man cannot live without belief. Everybody believes in something. Yet the basic problem in believing the positive is that we live in a negative world. We're conditioned to failure. The earth quakes, trees and stars fall, buildings collapse, tornados destroy, hurricanes devastate, tidal waves crush and people lie, cheat and steal.

To believe in the positive, we have to discipline ourselves away from the negative of the world. In studies and surveys of financially successful people, I have noticed that the most commonly recurring factors to which they attribute their success are:

- communication skills
- intelligence
- integrity
- experience
- a positive attitude

To believe positively, we must be converted from the negative. We must be taught not only to believe but to believe right.

What you believe shapes your life. Because it's basic to your choices, belief is the basis for conduct, character and destiny. Wrong conduct is based on wrong believing. Criminals believe they can get away with it; prisoners believe someone else put them there; substance abusers believe drugs give them a good time; and homosexuals believe they were made that way.

Fools say that there is no God, Scripture declares.[4] It's foolishness to believe there is no God and no accountability for our actions. We all give an account for our actions, one way or another. The sexually promiscuous are held accountable by disease, divorce, abortion and other assorted judgments; embezzlers, con artists and the like by law and, even more, by retribution.

Practical atheism is not raising a fist and shouting, "There is no God!" It's living as if there is none.

Contrast the lives just mentioned with the life of Daniel, a man who from his earliest youth adhered to belief in Jehovah God, trusted in the Scriptures and relied on prayer. That lifestyle became the basis for elevation to the second-highest office in the land. Righteousness causes goodness and mercy to follow a man all his life.

Maxwell Maltz, a plastic surgeon and author, studied psychocybernetics because of the attitude of his patients after plastic surgery. Interestingly, what they believed about themselves before and after surgery determined whether they accepted or rejected themselves and his work. He found it necessary to work as much on their beliefs as on their bodies in order to be successful.

What you believe determines your relationships—not just with others, but foremost with yourself. How you see yourself bears on the relationship you have with others. What you believe has the power to attract or repel. If you believe God is capricious, condemnatory and censorious, it will repel you from belief in Him and the Bible. But if you believe what the Bible reveals Him to be—a loving Father, wonderful Savior and gracious Lord—your attraction to Him will know no bounds.

Faith and Fear

Faith is simply an extension of belief, because it is believing that what you cannot see will come to pass. Fear is likewise an extension of belief, believing that what you cannot see will come to pass. Both faith and fear have the same definition, but faith attracts the positive, while fear attracts the negative.

Whatever you believe, whether true or not, is real to you. If you believe it, it doesn't matter whether it's based on truth, perception, fantasy or hearsay—you believe it, so it's real to you. Men can gamble throughout their lives, believing that any day they'll "hit the big one," and it's real to them. Then they wonder why their wives leave, why they have trouble at work and what's wrong with their relationships. Their beliefs are working against them. Others fear that someone is "out to get them" and withdraw, emotionally or physically, to protect themselves from pain or loss. Such cases prove that "as [a man] thinketh in his heart, so is he."[5]

Unbelief is the most expensive commodity in life.

Years ago, I worked with a man named John who was extremely successful. He thought expansively, dreamed of big things and seemed to accomplish every goal. When I met him, he was financially "set" and dreaming of doing "great things for God."

A media deal came up whereby John could invest in an avenue of ministry that was new and exciting. He envisioned great returns, doing something no one had done before and expanding the Kingdom of God almost single-handedly. Financially, however, it became a heavier burden than he had anticipated, and he began to look for ways to sustain the venture.

During that time, a lady called to meet him. She was, she said, the heiress to a large fortune, and she wanted to make John her beneficiary so he could accomplish all he dreamed and more. Believing he was on a "mission from God" and now enabled by God, even without seeing any proof of the woman's financial substance, he began to base his actions on her promises.

John's staff and godly counselors around him warned him that her wealth appeared to be a figment of his imagination, that this woman was deceiving herself and deceiving him and that if he didn't stop his wild spending, he would lose everything. But he had become so enamored of the dreams the multiplied millions would bring about that he refused to believe it could not be true. It was real to him, so he refused to believe otherwise.

When creditors began to call for unpaid bills and John's reserves were depleted, he asked the woman for an "advance" on the estate. First came delays, and then she stopped returning his calls. Soon she stopped even receiving them, and suddenly, she was gone. John's belief in a lie and unbelief in obvious truth caused him to lose everything he had accumulated over the years. It was tragic for him and those who depended upon him. His demise did not need to happen, but it did and only because he rejected godly counsel and believed a lie. Yoked to a lie by unbelief in truth, he bore the burden of losing all.

Jesus said, "Take my yoke upon you, and learn of me ... For my yoke is easy, and my burden is light."[6] Christ's figure of speech referred to the carts that passed through town in His day pulled by animals yoked together. Harnessed to that yoke, the animals were burdened with the heavy load they pulled. Jesus was counseling us to yoke to Him in our believing, because His burden is light. That principle holds true in every area of life.

Students who are yoked to believing they can't learn are burdened with ignorance, failure and despair. That's a heavy burden for anyone to bear through life. On the other hand, pupils yoked to believing they can learn and even excel are "burdened" with knowledge, satisfaction and self-esteem. That's a burden carried easily.

People yoked to the belief that it's desirable and pleasurable to live fast, to beat everyone and to triumph in multiple sexual encounters, carry the burden of shallow relationships, stalled careers and failed health. Too often they also live on the edge of paranoia. Because of their belief in their lustful, "swinging" lifestyle, they are yoked to an insatiable desire that does not allow fulfillment or peace.

Marrying a woman in Christian faith is a yoke that carries the "burden" of rich intimacy, responsible maturation, deep unity and strong character. The love in such a relationship grows richer, sweeter and deeper as the years go by. Because that love emanates from an eternal source, it never grows old or wears out. The burden is ever light.

Choosing a career that God has purposed for you is a yoke that carries the "burden" of deep fulfillment, great achievement and long-lasting productivity.

The yoke of rejecting Jesus carries a burden of guilt, fear and hiding. Believing on Him carries a "burden" of righteousness, peace and joy.

Trusting God as the author of your efforts brings the "burden" of knowing He will finish them. Whatever God authors, He will complete. Whatever God promises, He will fulfill. Whatever is committed to Him, God will keep.

The strength of such belief is a persuasion "that neither death, nor life, nor angels, nor principalities, nor powers, nor things present, nor things to come, nor height, nor depth, nor any other creature, shall be able to separate us from the love of God, which is in Christ Jesus our Lord."[7]

Daniel could face the lions calmly with the stability of his trust in a faithful God.

Choices Have Consequences

We recently held one of our Christian Men's Events in Reno, Nevada, a city that glamorizes gambling and prostitution. During the course of the day, I mentioned to the men that preaching never gets easier for me. At times, I agonize when I think of something I said, didn't say or said wrong in presenting the message that Christ is Lord. Sometimes when I'm "at home" in a strange hotel room after speaking to men all day, I have cried on my pillow, knowing some men left the place without the knowledge of Christ's saving grace and power.

When we wrapped up the meeting and I started for the door, a man caught my arm. He was rough-looking, but as I sized him up, I saw a glimmer in those red-rimmed eyes and a glow around his haggard face. In a raspy voice he said, "You don't have to cry tonight. I'm the last one in my family to receive Christ, and I did it today." Then his eyes brimmed with tears, and he quickly walked away. I slept in peace that night.

Choices determine destiny.

Choices determine destiny.

Opportunities are doors of choices that open for our benefit. Many men miss their opportunities or don't realize when they have them, and they go their way without realizing what awaited them. Later, they see what could have been theirs. It's better to pray to be ready for opportunities when they come than to pray they come.

Such is the case with men who don't seize the opportunity to believe on Jesus Christ and go their way without realizing they are living far below the level God created for them. Man's highest level is in the heavenly places in Christ Jesus. Nothing tops it.

Resolving to serve God means more than taking the family to church on Sundays. It's more than a desire to give up bad habits, foul language or immoral fantasies. Those plans are mere human purposes, and when they are not kept, they result in guilt and condemnation. But a resolve to serve God is from the heart and spirit. It's a determination to be faithful, regardless of what happens. It takes courage to be a Christian.

Too often, Christians are called "wimpy" when just the opposite is true. Persevering in devotion to the Lord takes far more manhood than sitting back in judgment on the Church, deriding Christianity and joining those who reject Christ. The easiest way becomes the hardest.

Sometimes, because of a limited view of Christians and miniscule knowledge of the Gospel, men do not understand what they are doing when they refuse Jesus Christ. Some who have heard and even mentally accepted the Gospel still turn away because they haven't established themselves in Christ and His Word. Their decision was one of convenience, not conviction.

To stand for righteousness when others bow to the world's pressure makes a man taller than the rest.

- When a man refuses Christ, he robs Heaven of his presence even though God wants him there, Christ paid the price for him there, and God has sent His Holy Spirit to help prepare him for life there. In refusing Christ and inhibiting his family from faith in God, he has become his own and their messiah. He has taken the place of God in their lives and become their "lord who provides." He becomes the counterfeit trinity–"me, myself and I."

- When a man refuses Christ, he robs the Church of his contribution of life and influence, weakening it by his absence and hindering others from entering in. He also robs his community, which needs his moral and spiritual support. Community values can come only from the moral absolutes implanted in the individual's life through God's Word and Spirit.

- To refuse Christ is to call God a liar. It's man's word against His. Scripture states, "He who does not believe God [in this way] has made Him out to be and represented Him as a liar, because he has not believed (put his faith in, adhered to, and relied on) the evidence (the testimony) that God has borne regarding

His Son."[8] Refusing Christ shows disdain for God's Word. Choosing man's word over God's impugns God's character.

- Refusing Christ makes a man a participant in Satan's anarchy against God. Refusing Christ aligns a man with those destined for Hell, which the Bible says is being enlarged to receive them.[9]

- A man refusing Christ lives on a level below what God intended, is a slave to desires he doesn't like, is ruled by spirits that hate him and is destined to be lost to the presence of God for eternity. Hell is a place without light because God is light, and He is not there. There is no love, mercy or forgiveness; no satisfaction or fulfillment; no companionship, friendship or any relationship that's not based on rebellion. Hell is filled with pain, sorrow, tears and the memory of lost opportunities that constantly torment its inhabitants. In contrast, Heaven is a place of light, love, grace, mercy, forgiveness; friends and family for eternity; total personal fulfillment; no sorrow, pain or tears; memories only of righteousness and what was good and perfect; where we live in the presence of God and are continuously filled with the glory of God. Hallelujah!

Now consider this: Having treated God's Word with disdain, called God a liar throughout life, taken God's place in others' lives and supported Satan against God—what makes a man think that when he dies, God is going to receive him into Heaven? A man lives a life dishonoring to God and then expects God to honor him. Isn't that incredible? Yet men believe it.

It takes courage to repent and believe on Jesus. It's humbling to admit to someone you've scorned, mocked or threatened that their way is the right way, their God the right God. It takes guts to make the decision. For that reason, God's Spirit is here to give us the strength of resolve to repent and the power to live godly lives.

Why be one of the crowd who lacks courage or resolve to serve Christ? Why follow the popular course instead of being a man whom God can point to as His workmanship? God takes great pleasure in a man's faith in Him.

It's going to take a lot of manliness to weather the coming storms of life. The first, most important resolution is to believe on the Lord Jesus Christ with all your heart. Once that's resolved, the rest of what you need becomes almost simple because the Holy Spirit of God living in you will help you accomplish all God has for you.

Resolve to believe God, regardless of the people or circumstances around you. Yoke yourself to belief in Jesus Christ, and accept the light burden He alone can give.

End Thoughts

- The discipline of daily devotion to God undergirds decisions.
- Perseverance will always outlast persecution.
- A person's beliefs hold the greatest potential for good or harm in life.
- Wrong conduct is based on wrong beliefs.
- What you believe is the basis for conduct, character and destiny.
- Whatever God authors, He will complete. Whatever God promises, He will fulfill. Whatever is committed to Him, God will keep.
- It's better to pray to be ready for opportunities when they come than to pray they come.
- The counterfeit trinity is "me, myself and I."

Reflections

1. Have you ever had a belief that harmed you?
2. What have you believed about God in the past? Has it changed? What do you believe about Him today?
3. Is there any reason not to believe God is who He says He is? Do you believe God is a good God who is willing to make you a strong man and a hero?

THREE

MY BROTHER'S KEEPER

Show me a man's companions, and I'll show you his character.

A man stood up on the last day of our recent Leadership Training Institute and told us about the most remarkable part of the entire week: For the first time in his life, he felt as if he was among friends. His Christian walk had been a lonely one, but he left with the understanding of the necessity to "show" himself friendly.[1]

One striking aspect of the account of Daniel is his relationship with his three closest friends. His companions are commonly called the "three Hebrew children," and they were true heroes— "teen-men" who were almost recklessly willing to die for their beliefs. Daniel and his three young friends were taken captive together and supported each other in their decision to serve the Lord God. Each of them had an uncommon faith, held an uncommon standard and underwent an uncommon test.

When Daniel rose to power in Babylon, his three friends were given provinces of the country to administrate as well. But theirs was not an easy road. When the king built an image of himself and required the entire nation to worship it, Daniel's friends refused. As a result, they were thrown into a furnace so hot that it killed those who were stoking the fire. Refusing to recant their convictions, believing that God could deliver them even from certain death (but not doubting Him if He didn't, as theirs was Heaven to gain), they were tied and thrown into the furnace.

The king watched them go, thinking he'd see them writhe in pain and burn. Instead, he was astonished to see them walking about in the flames—joined by a Heaven-sent fourth man!

When the king called to them, the three walked out from the flames unsinged, without even the smell of smoke on their clothes. Strengthened through godly friendship, bonded in the fire together, they stood now as heroes. Some people attribute this account to Bible "mythology." But it isn't so hard to believe. It's a far smaller deed to God to save a man physically from the flames of death than to save him spiritually from the eternal fire of Hell.

In our present society, the greatest acts of genocide occur in history books, newspapers, magazines, TV and films, where our heroes are killed with gossip, slander, exposé and innuendo. On the one hand, our would-be heroes are denuded and dishonored by writers who scrutinize their lives and motives based on a standard to which they themselves cannot adhere. On the other hand, those who break laws, engage in titillating yet grossly immoral deeds or flagrantly rebel against constituted authority are written about in magazines and books and given television airtime in movies or special news programs. In the midst of such bombardment from the evil side of human nature, our society needs strong men who have faith in God and in their brethren.

Soldiers are trained to trust their buddies and superiors in combat. At times, that trust has been misplaced through cowardice, abandonment or fraud on the part of the compatriot, but it doesn't stop trained troops from continuing in service. The failure of one person doesn't stop us from believing in another.

Likewise, being a "soldier of the cross" in the war zone of our world today means not stopping with one failure. Though a fellow trooper stops, still others march on. Though one minister falls, still thousands stand strong. Though one friend fails, still others remain true. Though we ourselves falter, still we press on.

The Faith of a Friend

In the tough times that Barnabas lived through during the time period covered by the Book of Acts, he held fast to his faith in God and in a friend and relative. "Barnabas ... was a good man, and full of the Holy Ghost and of faith," the Bible records.[2]

Barnabas was a contemporary of Saul, the zealot who rapidly persecuted the Church, hauling men and women to prison and even putting some to death. Saul met Christ on a remote road to Damascus, which radically changed the course of his life. The experience was so phenomenal, the brightness of the presence of the Lord so brilliant, that Saul was transformed from an arch persecutor of the Lord into an ardent disciple. Barnabas soon became Saul's mentor. He introduced Saul to the Church he formerly persecuted, and he worshipped God with him for many years as the Lord prepared Saul for ministry under his new name, Paul. Barnabas was again tapped by God, this time to be Apostle Paul's first traveling companion in missionary work.

The excitement surrounding their first voyage must have been intense. To assist them, a young man was chosen–a nephew of Barnabas' named John Mark. Mark's mother, Mary, hosted the Jerusalem church in her home. They were evidently long-time followers of Christ, for most theologians agree that Mark was as eyewitness to the betrayal and arrest of Jesus in the Garden of Gethsemane. Because of Mark's familiarity with the Gospel and heart for ministry, he was chosen for that exciting adventure in faith with Paul and Barnabas.

The missionary trip was grueling. Faced with difficult circumstances, Mark decided midway through the journey to return to Jerusalem. The other missionaries completed their arduous and prosperous venture and returned home with great reports of people believing in Christ and churches being established.

After some time, Barnabas and Paul decided to go out again. Barnabas wanted to take John Mark with them, but Paul objected. Mark had failed in his first test. Paul was not keen on giving him another opportunity. The contention between the two men concerning Mark became so sharp that they decided to separate.

Paul chose Silas as his new helper and continued his journeys. From their work, churches were established, and much of the New Testament was written. Barnabas, on the other hand, is not mentioned again in the narrative of the book of Acts. Barnabas was lost to history after his great part in Paul's salvation and ministry. But was his challenge to Paul worth it? Was he right or wrong to have faith in his nephew even though Mark had failed the first time?

The young John Mark went on to become a historian. He conducted interviews, recorded the events of the life of Jesus Christ and wrote under the inspiration of the Holy Spirit. Without his writings, which scholars believe were the foundation for others, we may not have had the books of Matthew, Luke and John. Because of Barnabas, we have four complete Gospels.

Was Barnabas' faith in Mark worthwhile? Yes! His faith was further vindicated when Paul wrote later, "Get Mark and bring him with you, for he is very helpful to me for the ministry."3 Barnabas didn't quit on Mark. Neither did God. Barnabas was strong in faith–in God and in men of God.

By losing his life, Barnabas found greater glory. He ministered to hundreds or perhaps thousands, and two to whom he ministered, Paul and Mark, have ministered to billions for hundreds of years. His dedicated investment paid dividends beyond anything he could have imagined.

We must have faith in others and in God's work in their lives in order to make it through tough times. God said that all of us who identify with Christ are collectively the Body of Christ. We need to move and flow as one unit. God will bring those godly friends into your life who will stand with you through the hard times. Daniel had his three intimate friends. John Mark had his Uncle Barnabas. Paul, the apostle, had Silas and other Christian brothers. God strengthens us through our friends.

The Substance Called Faith

Once when I was younger, my itinerary took my family and me through the country around Niagara Falls. There I heard what became one of my favorite illustrations of faith. It's the true story of the tightrope walker who announced that he would walk across Niagara Falls. The day came for the feat to be accomplished. A huge crowd jammed both the Canadian and American sides. The wire was mounted and strung across the falls.

Standing on the American side, the man yelled to the crowd, "Does anyone believe I can cross the falls, holding just this balancing pole?"

We must have faith in others and in God's work in their lives, in order to make it through tough times.

No one answered.

Up on the wire he went and then across the falls. When he reached the Canadian side, the people cheered enthusiastically, perhaps from relief. "Does anyone here believe I can do it again?" he asked the Canadians.

Having seen it, numbers of them raised their hands and cheered.

Then he asked, "How many believe I can do it, holding this chair?" He held a chair aloft, and few people raised their hands or called out.

Again he walked across the deep gorge with its terrifying, rushing waters. Those on the American side shouted and whistled with thunderous applause. When the noise subsided, he asked, "How many believe I can cross it with a wheelbarrow?"

This time the majority of the crowd raised their hands and cheered wildly.

"OK," said the tightrope walker, "who will be the first to get in?"

No one raised a hand. It was one thing to applaud someone who risked his own life but quite another to put yourself in that wheelbarrow. Applauding was an act of *belief*. Getting into the wheelbarrow was an act of *faith*.

Enthusiasm is an emotion. Optimism is an attitude. Faith is a substance.[4]

How strong is your faith? Attending church, singing hymns and reading a psalter when times are easy and everyone is doing it is one thing; but what of the times when your very nature is going to be tested to the core?

You strengthen your faith *now*, not when you need it. You prepare for the testing time. It's like insurance. You don't buy it after you become ill; you buy it when you're well. Now is the time. Turn your belief into faith by acting upon it.

Daniel's life of devotion to his beliefs prepared him for the lions' den. The three Hebrew children would never have taken the stand they did without being deeply rooted in God's Word by faith. We don't know how strong our faith is until we're tested. God tests us in order to prove us. He sets us up for success, not failure.

Scripture says that if we wait for perfect conditions, we will never do anything.[5] I started all over again five times in five years, making new friends, developing new relationships, hearing from God anew. Hearing from God doesn't depend on age but on relationship. You are never too old ... and you're never too young.

Even though you may feel like a fool when you're around some people, and even though many others may have let you down, millions of people have never even heard of you! They don't know your mistakes or failures. Nor have their mistakes or failures reached you. Don't let the few hinder you. Have faith in God!

The Greater Faith

As important as it is to have faith in God, there's an element of faith even greater than that—God has faith in men! I will never forget a story I heard years ago about God's faith. It was told to me by one of the finest men I ever met, W. T. Gaston. As a young man and leader in the revival of that day, he was an eyewitness to the event.

In those days, the custom of God-fearing evangelistic groups was to have "brush arbor meetings." The name came from making meeting places by sticking poles in the ground, then stringing wires or rope from pole top to pole top and placing branches of bushes across and over the wires to give shade during the day and cover by night. They would nail planks together to make outdoor seating, and worshippers would gather for morning, afternoon and evening meetings. Often, they would go out into the neighboring community to evangelize and bring new converts or interested parties to the meetings. It wasn't uncommon for them to bring pup tents for shelter and cots for beds so they could stay as late as they wanted to "tarry" in prayer services. Much fasting, shouting and singing, preaching and praying took place from morning to night.

At one such meeting, one of the worship leaders went to his cot to rest at noontime. The gentleman was in the tenth day of a fast, and as he dozed in the heat of the day, he saw a vision.

In the vision, he was standing on the Mount of Olives in the back of a large crowd. He could barely see over the people's heads. An absolute quietness reined, a stillness so deep that not even the shuffle of a foot could be heard. Suddenly, he saw the head of a man appearing over the heads of the multitude. Then he saw the man's shoulders, finally His torso, and then He rose into the air. He watched in awe until Jesus was obscured by a small cloud. He was witnessing by vision the ascension of Jesus Christ.

Suddenly, in his vision, he was transported to a heavenly place where the first angels were coming to meet the Son of God. As the angels approached, he heard the first one ask, "Master, how did it go on earth?"

"Men will be saved," was the answer.

Jesus held up His hands, and the angels saw the scars on His hands, feet, side and brow where He sacrificed Himself for mankind's sin.

Because angels are ministering spirits, another question came. "But how will men know of their salvation?"

"I have commissioned My disciples to preach the good news in all the world," was the reply.

The angels rejoiced, but then, in concern, they asked, "But what if they fail?"

Jesus answered simply, "I have no other plan."

That was a vision, not holy writ. It was something someone experienced in the midst of the day and into the intensity of a fast. But hear what was said. God put His faith in mankind. God has faith in *you*!

End Thoughts

- God doesn't quit on you; don't quit God.
- When you limit yourself, you limit God; when you limit God, you limit yourself.
- Belief is not faith until it is acted upon.
- Enthusiasm is an emotion. Optimism is an attitude. Faith is a substance.
- God tests us in order to prove us. He sets us up for success, not failure.
- Hearing from God doesn't depend on age but on relationship.
- Have faith in God; God has faith in you.

Reflections

1. Who is the most faithful or trustworthy friend you have had? Have any friends been unfaithful or untrustworthy?
2. Has a past relationship or failure bothered you? Has it kept you from trying again?
3. Can you name three friends or potential friends who encourage and help build your faith in God? What can you do to pursue those friendships?

FOUR

DARING DISCIPLINE

The Rev. Avery Dulles, an influential Roman Catholic theologian and veteran of international ecumenical affairs, said in a recent article that two visions of the American political experiment are struggling for supremacy. The once-prevailing view is that democratic rule depends on people recognizing God-given principles of justice and morals. But that view is now pitted against one that says the nation is not bound to any fixed truths or morality.

The recognition that healthy self-government relies on acceptance of common moral standards is withering away. "Ultimately this could bring the collapse of democracy," Dulles concluded.[1]

It's ironic that democracy in the United States is waning while nations who adopted democratic principles instituted by the United States proliferate and now live more freely than Americans. While all the world is suffering from changing value systems, the United States is caught in a "culture war" that threatens the nation's political heritage.

Culture Has Consequences

It's going to take more than a good Sunday School record for men to overcome the consequence of the increasingly godless culture around them. As Senator Dan Coats of Indiana said, "This crisis of values is not a marginal issue pursued by moralists and leftover Puritans. It is central to the health and success of individuals. It is also central to the health and future of economic and social institutions. The character of our children is the leading indicator of our future as a culture ... when our children are sick of soul, there is no higher priority than to seek their healing."[2]

Much of the violence done to common moral standards begins in the home. We see violence in children everywhere. "Families are the school of first instruction," Senator Coats said.[3] Yet children growing up without strong and positive parental influence succumb to control by the baser sorts of society that allow them the short-term luxury of living without discipline.

Pat, a pastor friend of mine, helped me in a recent Christian Men's Event. As we were leaving the building, a man stopped us and asked for help. He related some facts about problems he had in his job, with his family and with his life in general. "Even my eighteen-year-old son is a problem," he said to finish his litany of difficulties. "He keeps bringing his girlfriend home and insists on her staying overnight with him."

I looked at him in amazement, hardly trusting myself to speak. "What?" I managed to reply.

"He says that if we don't let him bring her home, he'll leave, and my wife says he's not old enough to leave yet," he stated blankly.

We stood there and just looked at each other, with him waiting for an answer and me waiting to see if Pat would answer first. Fortunately, he did.

"Man, don't you know you set the standard in the home?" Pat began. "As long as your son is at home, he is to live by your standards. Your son is committing fornication under your roof, and you're permitting it. No wonder you're having problems. You're living under the curse and not God's blessing. You're being a double-minded man, and you're unstable in all your ways."[4]

"What can I do about it?" he asked sincerely.

"Be a man!" Pat said.

I listened carefully as Pat spoke, and now it was my turn. "You need to exercise authority in your home," I explained. "Not dictatorially, but with true leadership. I've said this before, and I'll say it to you now—being nice is not always being loving.

"By being nice to your son, you are letting him do what's wrong. That's not loving. Your son is stronger in rebellion than you are in righteousness. You've allowed your son's lusts to grow stronger than your love for God."

With a look of determination, the result of which we may never know, he turned to head for home.

The Traits of True Love

Love is not license. True love has restraints. It will do no evil. Lust, on the other hand, has no limits to doing evil. There's an eternity between love and lust. Love is the spirit of Heaven, lust of Hell.

The strong men we've talked about all exhibit seven characteristics of love that accompany salvation:

- love of the Lord
- love of the brethren
- love of the Word
- love of the Lord's fellowship (worship and prayer)
- love of service
- love of the church
- love of ministry (ministers)

If we are people of love, serving a God who Himself is love, the love of God within us will result in restrained behavior. Our self-discipline as believers is born out of our love for God.

We discipline ourselves to study the Word of God because we love God. Likewise, we discipline children because we love them, not because we're angry with them. We discipline ourselves to exercise because we love ourselves and want healthy minds and bodies, not because we hate ourselves. We discipline ourselves to make a living because we love the family we're supporting.

When we're self-disciplined, it's easy to bring discipline into the home. The home is a microcosm of the community. Failure to adhere to standards in the home will allow for failure in public life.

Love limits behavior. Love for God limits evil-doing. Religion as a whole limits behavior in a society. Because of the strength of a moral standard, segments of our society today are attempting to do away with religion, or to render it powerless (without influence on society), so they can exercise their carnal lusts and live lasciviously.

For example, many who are influential and famous in Hollywood and journalism either engage in, are enamored of or empathize with immorality. These people make every effort to stigmatize Christianity as being mean-spirited, hypocritical or bigoted, and they use methods both subtle and covert to communicate their distorted views of society. They attach "Bible" or "Christian" to film characters who are weird, hard-hearted, implacable, legalistic or perverted.

The prodigal son in Christ's parable descended by stages to a level below that of animals. The first stage of his rebellion was a desire for independence. He didn't want to live by his father's standards or be subject to his father's will. No longer restrained by the presence of his father, his conscience no longer bothered by a mother's love, the prodigal was free from all moral restraints. The result was a descent into a degraded life. You pay to stray. There's always a high price for low living.

The Blame Game

It's easier for the guilty to blame others as the cause of negative consequences rather than accept and live with blame themselves. Demetrius, the silversmith from the Book of Acts, did this. When Christianity prospered and people began to worship the true God, they broke their idols and burned their pagan books. The source of financial gain for Demetrius and those of his trade was the ability to create idols of the goddess Diana. When Christians forswore her worship, the silversmiths' cash cow was gone. In his fury at the loss of his livelihood, Demetrius created an uprising to try to put away both Christians and Christianity. His lust for money was the root of his evil.

History is replete with such instances. Nero blamed the Christians for the burning of Rome. History says he played the fiddle and rejoiced as the multitudes sought to kill the Christians.

Guilt is a killer. It burdens the conscience, weighs on the spirit and deadens relationships. To eliminate guilt, the cause must be eliminated. Eventually, the prodigal repented, eliminating the cause and therefore the guilt. Many do not. Rather than face responsibility for sin, many blame those whose upright lifestyle ever reminds them of their own failure. The Bible talks about people who not only take delight in the base things of this world, but also applaud others who think up new ways to behave even more lasciviously.[5] They even hold awards ceremonies to honor their new inventions of wickedness.

Lenin said he would not speak of being an atheist but instead would speak of religion as an entirely private matter. If Christianity can be privatized, it can then be penalized and ultimately criminalized. That pattern prevailed in the communist Soviet Union and Romania. There are symptoms of it in America. *It will make for tough times.*

It's getting tough when ...

- in New York, six homosexual/abortion radicals committed vile acts as they interrupted Cardinal O'Connor's Mass in Saint Patrick's Cathedral. They trashed the host, chained themselves to pews, hurled condoms, spouted obscenities during his sermon and fell limp in the aisles. They were sentenced to community service without fine or penalty.[6]
- a man simply blocked the entrance to an abortion clinic and was fined $25,000 and ordered to pay $157,000 in lawyers' fees.[7]
- a schoolgirl's religious materials were taken from her by her teacher, then thrown away by the principal who told her mother, "I will not have religious materials on my campus." Yet humanism and revisionist history pervade our school textbooks.[8]
- homosexuals invaded church grounds, barricaded church members in the building by blocking the doors, threw stones at those who tried to enter and traumatized the members' children by taunting, "We

want your children. Give us your children." Yet the very next year a Florida District Court ruled that a religion-free "buffer zone" could be established around an abortion clinic, allowing only pro-abortion rhetoric—meaning that on public streets and sidewalks, homosexuals can terrorize Christians, but Christians cannot peaceably protest the killing of the unborn.[9]

- a college student was fired from his job as a resident adviser for talking in the dorm about his Christian faith.[10]
- an alcohol rehabilitation nurse was fired for "violating word rules" by praying with patients to the "higher power" they were told to believe in.[11]

Enough little raindrops make a flood. These are only a few of the myriad incidents occurring in America daily. It's called *prosecution*. Prosecution means *persecution* to Christians. It is not new to those who go by the Name of Christ. They have suffered ever since Christ was crucified.

Persecution of Christians is just an attempt to rid the world of Jesus Christ, which can't be done. Satan tried it and couldn't do it. Others have also tried it and failed.

Nicolae Ceausescu of Romania vowed to rid his nation of Christianity, and through despotic greed, he led his people into abysmal depths of poverty. He was assassinated on Christmas Day—a fitting irony. What brought his downfall started with one lone, obscure Christian pastor who refused to bow to the evil dictator's edicts. The pastor was a strong man in those tough times.

The pastor's godly convictions proved stronger than Ceausescu. Such convictions, with a force that can shape culture and change world history, do not come overnight. They are built line upon line, precept upon precept. The decision to believe on Jesus Christ that begins the building process may not seem like much at the time, but it's the start. The Bible warns us not to despise the day of small beginnings.

Developing Discipline

Daniel's decisions started when he was a teen-man. When he was taken from Israel to Babylon and selected to be trained by King Nebuchadnezzar's leading advisers, he and his friends were told they must dine at the king's table. Daniel requested instead to eat the food of his culture, not that of the king. Daniel found favor with the king's chamberlain, who gave temporary permission for Daniel and his friends to practice their religious beliefs regarding food. When the chamberlain found, days later, that Daniel and his friends were in better health than the others because of their diet, he allowed them to continue. This small decision became the basis for other decisions that caused Daniel to rise to the head of government in that foreign land.

Daniel's practice of adhering to a strict diet and to fasting is not unusual for men of spiritual strength. Jesus Himself said prayer and fasting were necessary to cast out certain demonic spirits.[12] The power of the Spirit of God in the believer must be stronger than that in the demonically possessed. Fasting is a way to gain spiritual strength.

"Better to rule the spirit than take a city," the Proverb says.[13] The rule Daniel had over his spirit took him a long way.

"Forasmuch as an excellent spirit, and knowledge, and understanding, interpreting of dreams, and showing of hard sentences, and dissolving of doubts, were found in the same Daniel ...."[14] Because of this kind of reputation, Nebuchadnezzar called for Daniel. "I have even heard of thee," the king said, "that the spirit of the gods is in thee, and that light and understanding and excellent wisdom is found in thee."[15] Daniel had within him something that, apart from God, man does not have.

God created man with a spirit, soul and body. In the soul, He gave us our minds, wills and emotions. The will is the center of man's determinate action and the place where purposes are established.

The Seventh Sense

I believe, in creation, man was given five physical senses plus a sixth sense in his mentality. Mankind's mentality must have been extremely powerful because Adam was able to name everything that was created. That mental gift became blighted by sin, and, as a result, much of its power has been lost.

It is my personal conviction that we were also given a seventh sense in the spirit. Above and more powerful than the other six senses, it's an ability to receive God's Spirit and develop His characteristics to some extent—to be able to think God's thoughts, feel God's feelings, say God's words and work God's works. This was part of original creation but was also lost through sin. Restored through Christ, this spiritual awareness is the source of power in believers' lives.

When living in Northern California, I developed a close relationship with a fine gentleman. When Charles was developing his contracting business, he signed to build a shopping center for a large firm. He went to his office early on the morning they were to start construction. While getting the plans and instruments packed in his car, hurrying to be ready to meet the men when they arrived for work, he had a nagging sensation in his spirit. It troubled his mind. The urge to pray was strong, yet he had to get on the job.

Giving in, he knelt at his chair behind his desk to pray, and while he prayed, the Holy Spirit quickened his thinking. A sudden picture flashed into his mind of the men who had surveyed the property. It troubled him, but he didn't know why. The thought occurred that he should double-check it by surveying the site himself before starting the project.

That morning, he discovered the survey was wrong on the back property line, where it was almost two feet off the mark. He checked it again, had his foreman verify his finding, then changed the markers to conform to what the "specs" called for. Busy, he forgot to mention the matter to anyone, and it slipped his mind entirely as the days went by.

When finally the project was finished, Charles was waiting for his final payment from the developer. He called the developer, who told him he could not give Charles his final payment because the construction was in error. It was all built too close to the property line. Immediately, Charles called for meetings with all responsible parties. En route, he remembered the survey he had taken, went back to get the papers and, in the meeting. showed what had happened. All the work was completed properly. He received his final payment.

Charles had received direction in that seventh sense in his spirit, given by the indwelling Spirit of God. By being "led by the Spirit," he overcame a potential misfortune.

Spiritual strength gives authority over the downward pull toward things earthy and merely human. Man was created from the dust of the earth, and all his sustenance stems from it. Our idioms of speech regard immoral or unlawful things as "earthy" or "dirty." We refer to vulgar jokes as being "dirty." Sin gave man a downward direction. We "fall" into sin and "stoop" to something "low." Unethical practices are "beneath" us, and we can "hit bottom." This earthiness is natural to man unless something draws him upward, away from such base elements.

Long after Adam's first sin, we read Apostle Paul's list of the "works of the flesh," which are qualities that have succumbed to a downward pull.[16] In the absence of God in our lives, we are naturally dragged downward toward these "beggarly elements."[17] But when Christ made it possible for us to receive the Spirit of God again, via the new birth, we also received His resurrection power in our spirits, enabling us to live "above" or have power over the lusts of the flesh.

A new creation in Christ Jesus has a power the unregenerate can't imagine. To have "the mind of Christ" and to be "led by the Spirit of God" is to be able to think, act and be motivated by that seventh sense.[18] It's supernatural! It's also why unbelievers are so frustrated with Christians. Believers live on a higher plane. Living there takes the work of faith and the discipline of the mind and body, but that's a small price to pay for such a high life.

The Secret of Fasting

Jesus said these things "goeth not out but by prayer and fasting,"[19] meaning that we need to be alive in the Spirit realm as the "living soul" we were created to be. By walking in the Spirit, we are enabled to have a strength flowing from God–to think, feel, act and do what God desired; to exercise His authority on earth.[20]

Praying and fasting go together like a rod and reel.

To fast from food is symbolic of severing oneself from earthy things. In fasting, we cut off the supply from the earthy to the physical. At the same time, we increase the spiritual supply to the heart and mind, bringing the physical into subjection to the spiritual. This is the primary purpose and result of fasting.

Fasting from things other than food is likewise fundamentally sound–the television, newspaper, telephone–whatever keeps us umbilically attached to that which is earthy. When you fast from the earthy and, at the same time, devote yourself to reading the Word of God and prayer, you allow the Spirit to energize your spirit and bring your soul and body under subjection so that the presence of God increases in your life.

Fasting is such a basic principle that even when done naturally, it initiates great strength of spirit. Mahatma Gandhi knew this secret. The strength derived from fasting gave him power over men and nations. Journalists and celebrities have also found it to be a source of healing and power.

I realize this is stringent discipline, but we're talking about the kind of discipline it takes to make it through tough times. My wife, Nancy, and I have a friend, Lee Bueno, who was healed of an incurable disease through fasting.[21] Recently, a close friend by the name of Dawn spent some time in Lee's retreat center. On her return home, when Dawn walked off the airplane, her husband didn't even know her, she was so changed. There was a radiance, an openness, a beauty never apparent before.

Both Dawn and Lee were troubled for years until they combined their prayer with fasting. By applying themselves to the principles of the Bible concerning both, they found healing and a new life.

My own life was radically altered by God sovereignly instituting a forty-day fast in my life. I've never done it since, but that one time changed me forever. Every success I enjoy today was birthed during that fast.

I started keeping a diary once I realized what was happening. Little did I know the pattern in fasting. Everything God does is according to a pattern and based on a principle in His Kingdom. I learned those two axiomatic principles between the twenty-first and thirty-eighth days of the fast. As the Spirit of God took me from Genesis to Revelation in just days, the insights were startling. The first chapter of Genesis shows God's pattern of revelation through the world's creation. It always begins with a word from God and develops substance.

God gave a pattern for His tabernacle to Moses, for His temple to King David and for the Church to Apostle Paul. Daniel's prophecies were all undergirded by a divine pattern. *When men find God's pattern for their lives and base their faith on the principles in His Word, they become successful in all they do.* All the principles and promises of the Bible are the keys to the Kingdom.

The pattern for my fast was to take my breakfast, lunch and dinner hours to read the Bible and pray. The first few days, it was mostly reading until the mind and heart began to clear through repentance. As the days progressed, prayer became more real than ever, and faith took on a whole new dimension. Other than that, life went on normally with work and family. Around the twenty-first day, however, the Bible became so alive I could not read it enough. I was devouring it. Over time, repentance changed to supplication, then gave way to praise and then grew into intercession.

It may have been a once-in-a-lifetime experience, but it made an eternity of a difference. I don't advocate that anyone arbitrarily or unilaterally start a forty-day fast, but a pattern of fasting of some kind will intensify the spirit and fortify faith. (Study how to fast before beginning.)

Many men are willing to allow things to drag on, day in and day out—financial crises, marital crises, problems with work, kids, cars, friends—without disciplining themselves to get the mind or situation under control. Fasting is an obvious way to accomplish this.

Gaining Self-Discipline

At certain times, we need more power than we do in ordinary living. These times demand that we ruthlessly discipline ourselves. Whether to fight a cultural war, confess Christ at the risk of punishment, contest evil spirits or brave persecution—discipline is necessary. With your spirit under control, your heart subjected to God and your will set to please Him, you will then know the upward pull that overcomes the downward tug.

We live in a perverted world where man's will has been relegated to earthly purposes. For example, when God created Adam, He gave him dominion over the plants. But today plants are taking dominion over man. Cocaine, marijuana, alcohol and cigarettes, all derived from plants, have enslaved millions.

Man's will is able to do four things:
- weigh reasons
- balance motives
- pursue a fixed purpose
- choose either good or evil, right or wrong

We are born *in* sin and shaped in iniquity, but we were not born *to* sin. We are born to live righteously. Adam chose to obey Eve instead of God. Sin has always been a choice, an act of the will.

Besides the will, we also have a conscience that allows us to do two things:
- Pass judgment on ourselves
- Approve or condemn our own conduct

Spending time in the Word of God–reading, studying and memorizing–programs the conscience to think correctly concerning the world. Without submission to the Word of God, behavior can be rationalized to sanction any deed.

God purges our consciences from dead works at salvation.[22] The blood of Jesus, when applied, sprinkles our hearts from an evil conscience.[23] Apostle Paul, who once persecuted Christians, was able to live in all good conscience before God and man.[24]

Our wills and our consciences must be brought into subjection to God's will. He has the right, as the sovereign of our lives, to determine what is right and wrong for us. He will never ask us to do anything inconsistent with His will, contrary to His character or in opposition to His Word. The Spirit and the Word agree, so the Spirit will never lead us to do things the Word cannot confirm.

We can trust the will of God, because God always wills and works toward our highest good. Not believing this makes men hide from God, fearing His will for their lives. Prayerlessness is a form of hiding. We must discipline ourselves to overcome fear-fulness and to face God in prayer, allowing His will full reign in our lives.

This is the difference between men who discipline themselves and those who don't. Men who make disciplined decisions one after another–abiding in the Word, doing God's will–build within themselves a deeply-rooted, godly character that overcomes out-ward circumstances and devilish spirits. We call such people "men of conviction."

Strong men discipline themselves to the Word of God and prayer, to fasting when needed, to obedience to God's will. They are the men upon whom the world can depend. They are those to whom others run in tough times. They are the ones with the spirit of a Daniel who rise to greatness out of the smoldering ashes of their own ruined civilization, culture, crowd or career.

End Thoughts

- Being nice is not always being loving.
- Love is not license. True love has restraints.
- There is a high price for low living.
- Everything God does is according to a pattern and based on a principle of His Kingdom.
- The principles and promises of the Bible are the keys to the Kingdom.
- We are born *in* sin but not *to* sin.
- God will never ask us to do anything inconsistent with His will, contrary to His character or in opposition to His Word.
- Prayerlessness is a form of hiding.

Reflections

1. What events led up to the first time you ever realized you needed self-discipline?
2. How did self-discipline, fasting and prayer prepare Daniel for public life? for persecution?
3. In what way has the "seventh sense," or leading of the Holy Spirit, helped you in your occupation? family? a special problem you're having? What will you do this week to sharpen your awareness of the Holy Spirit's leading in your life?

FIVE

MEN MATURE

What's the difference between government bonds and men? Bonds mature.

How do you force a man to do sit-ups? Put the TV remote control between his toes.

Why is it a good thing there are women astronauts? When the crew gets lost in space, someone will ask for directions.

What does a man consider a seven-course meal? A hot dog and a six-pack.[1]

Sure, those are male-bashing jokes, and the sardonic humor is not lost on men. For years, we men have made everyone the butt of our humor—sick, black or vulgar—but to have women making fun of us and children laughing along is something else again.

Bonds mature? The meaning is not lost on us: Men don't automatically mature as they grow older. Maturity is measured by acceptance of responsibility. In the male, it's measured by responsibility in the God-given stewardship to guide, guard and govern. God gave Adam this three-fold responsibility in regard to earth. Every man since Adam has been charged with it.

Daniel's mature handling of the hardest issues of life marked him as a real man. By the time of his capture as a teenager, he had already become mature in knowledge gained as a child in Israel. He added to this the education of the king's house in Babylon, which must have been substantial. Babylon produced the Hanging Gardens, one of the great wonders of the ancient world, which indicates something of the wisdom of their culture.

Daniel's maturity was a personal process of development in a series of steps. The serious, disciplined and spiritually-minded approach in his tender teens produced the foundation for a lifetime of statesmanship. His depth of spirituality was revealed in a miracle that occurred while he was still young.

Daniel and his friends were in the king's house, being educated by men of letters. One day, the king called for all his wise men to interpret a dream. Cantankerous as he was, he insisted they not only give him the interpretation, but also tell him what the dream was, since he couldn't remember it. None could comply with his demand. As a result, all the wise men of the kingdom were sentenced to death.

When Daniel heard of their impending doom, he enlisted his friends to pray for revelation of the dream and its interpretation. The gift of dream interpretation God gave to Daniel that night was more than all the seers and prophets in the land could produce with their various human efforts. Of all Daniel's knowledge, the greatest could not be acquired from his teachers in Israel nor the wise men of Babylon–it was knowing the voice of God. That came from his life of devotion to the Lord.

When the day dawned and the wise men were to be slaughtered, Daniel volunteered to go to the king. He told the king the dream, gave the interpretation and saved scores of men's lives. He also secured his first position on the king's staff, as well as assignments for his three friends. His public life began as a result of the miracle.

The work of God does not come by the will of man, nor by the will of the flesh, but by the will of God. God is at work in a man's life both to will and to perform His good pleasure.[2] It was God's pleasure to answer Daniel and reveal secrets known only to Him.

Proverbs says God's secret is "with the righteous."[3] *God's good pleasure is to perform in each man that which fulfills his unique purpose and maximizes the potential of his life.*

Choosing Maturity

Two men I knew, Ray and Ben, went to work at the same time at a large Midwestern church. Both were in support positions in different departments of the large outreach. Both were from church backgrounds in other parts of the country. They were well versed on the manners and styles of Christian worship. Their new church was large in number and international in scope. The senior pastor was expansive in spirit, generosity, hospitality and vision. Both heartily congratulated themselves on landing jobs in such an exciting ministry, and their families were happy and proud of them.

Very quickly however, Ray felt overwhelmed by the freedom of worship other staff members exhibited at weekly staff prayer meetings. He felt ashamed of his lack of spiritual knowledge in comparison to other staff members and of his inability to join in conversations about the international church. He went home and began to thumb through his Bible to learn some passages he could contribute to prayer times. He subscribed to a Christian magazine and read portions of it for conversational material. He began to dress to

God's good pleasure is to perform in each man that which fulfills his unique purpose and maximizes the potential of his life.

impress his colleagues, bought jewelry for status symbols and occasionally used a Scripture reference in conversation. When working intimately at times with the pastor, he never took notes or made any effort to apply the teaching.

His boss, noticing his difficulty, took him to lunch several times and spent time praying with him to help him grow into his new position. Ray never did.

Ben, working in a different capacity, felt the same inferiority around the rest of the staff. He realized his spiritual immaturity in relation to them, and he recognized his was not a commitment to God but to church. With a troubled spirit, he asked his supervisor, an associate pastor, to lunch, and there he made his confessions. "I didn't know what I was getting myself into when you hired me," Ben said.

"How so?" the associate asked.

"Well, the way everyone prays out loud and talks constantly about all these missions around the world—I've never been around people like this."

"This is what this church stands for," his boss said. "I wondered if you might have difficulty assimilating it all. But I believe you know what to do about it."

"What?"

"Go back to your first love and find that relationship with the Lord that has grown stale. God desires to have a relationship with you. He wouldn't have brought you here otherwise. This is a big-spirited church with big-spirited employees."

Ben drove home that evening and gripped the steering wheel tightly. "I'm a small-spirited person," he cried in frustration. "I'm from a small-minded background. I have small visions and small desires, and I'm in way over my head because I'm–just–too–small!"

He thumped the steering wheel with the last three words. After dinner that night, he announced to his wife that he wouldn't join her for television because he had some important work to do. Alone in his room, he opened his Bible to page one and began to read. The stories were familiar, but he refused to skim or fall asleep. He continued his reading night after night, praying fervently for God to give him a big heart. Finally, he sensed a change. New meanings sprang to him out of remote passages about deserts, tabernacles and prophets. From the revelation came a new love for God, and prayer became more than a duty to perform.

Ben was renewed and began to enter into the larger spirit of the church. Ray, however, continued to drift, trying outwardly to impress while inwardly worrying that he'd be found out.

Both Ray and Ben were cut from the staff when the pastor had to "downsize," and Ray went back to a secular job. Ben was immediately offered a better church position elsewhere, however, with more pay and career advancement. He became an influence for righteousness and continued the maturing process he started when he was challenged.

Men who choose to mature, mature.

Levels of Life

Life is lived on levels and arrived at in stages. That's why the steps of a righteous man "are ordered by the Lord."4 Each step advances to a new level of responsibility, knowledge or authority and calls for further deepening of character. In spiritual growth, there is no retirement age.

Levels are not just vertical. An army marches horizontally, but its ranks have levels of responsibility: private, corporal, sergeant, lieutenant, captain, major, colonel, general. Each, in turn, represents a rise in rank, but they still march on the same terrain. Preachers and laymen often have different measures of divine revelation and responsibility, but both stand on the same ground of faith before God.

Maturity does not come with age but begins with the acceptance of responsibility. Accepting responsibility for your own sins and, by faith, asking forgiveness from God is the first step to spiritual maturity.

Men of God are exhorted to mature in the faith by a process. "Add to your faith virtue; and to virtue knowledge; And to knowledge temperance; and to temperance patience; and to patience godliness; And to godliness brotherly kindness; and to brotherly kindness charity."[5] True maturity begins with faith and culminates in charity, the full expression of love.

A lack of these is evidence that a person is spiritually immature. Either he has never been purged from sin, or he has forgotten about it. *The line of demarcation between those who have been purged and those still in their sins is at the cross of Christ.* The cross is man's source of all mercy and all true theological doctrine.

The cross is either man's greatest blessing or his worst curse. Knowing Christianity with a wisdom of words but without the power of God through the presence of the Holy Spirit and personal knowledge of Christ is to make the cross of no effect.

The cross is the source of man's greatest forgiveness or worst sin. Those who want the crown in Heaven without accepting the cross while on earth, who desire salvation by faith without repentance and who yearn for glory without grace are enemies of the cross.

The cross is the source of man's greatest glory and Satan's worst defeat. Our salvation was not bought with corruptible things such as silver and gold but was purchased by the precious blood of Jesus Christ. No wonder Apostle Paul cried, "God forbid that I should glory, save in the cross of our Lord Jesus Christ."[6]

To compromise the cross leads to deception, causes distraction, results in dislocation and ends in destruction. Millions are placed in that dangerous position constantly.

✳ Christ's death on the cross for the sins of mankind expressed the greatest maturity known to man. *It is one thing to accept responsibility for self, another to accept responsibility for others.* I once taught this in New Zealand, and a pastor left the meeting with new inspiration. He informed his congregation that he would accept responsibility for pastoring the entire community, not just the church membership. With that decision, he and his people accepted responsibility for their community, and the congregation more than doubled in a matter of months.

Man's pattern more often is to circumvent the cross of Christ. Of all the church members in America:

10% cannot be found;

20% never attend;

25% never pray;

30% never read the Bible;

40% never give to the church;

60% never give to world missions;

75% never assume a ministry service in the church;

95% have never won one person to Christ. Yet

100% expect to go to Heaven.[7]

To mature past the initial level of faith that provides salvation, men must return to the cross and add to their faith virtue, knowledge, temperance, patience, godliness, brotherly kindness and charity.

A renewing wave of God's Spirit swept over the world almost a generation ago and produced what has been referred to as the Charismatic Renewal. From that has sprung a plethora of new ministries, organizations and doctrines. Much good was accomplished. The emphasis on success that came out of that movement, however, tended to omit the cross and ignore repentance. The results have been confusion, difficulty and heartache as people have mistaken presumption for faith and human sorrow for godly sorrow.

Success in life is not the aim of the cross; it's the result of the cross.

A lifestyle of riches and fame is neither God's promise nor purpose. "Patched-up sinners" who retain their sin under a veneer of righteousness are not God's work. Confession is not all there is to conversion. God's Word is not a Band-Aid® for the fatal wound of sin. There's a difference between *renewal* and *revival*.

Conversely, prosperity is not the ten-letter obscenity portrayed by some who choose to live below their potential. Prosperity is the sequentially-ordered result of righteousness in one's life.[8]

> *Success in life is not the aim of the cross; it's the result of the cross.*

Satan made Jesus Christ an offer to gain all the kingdoms of this world without going to the cross. Jesus rejected his temptation because He knew the principle: "No cross, no crown." The cross is where you die to self and sin. "How shall we, that are dead to sin, live any longer therein?" the Scripture says.[9]

Many men who try to live a spiritually mature life have missed the first step. They've been taught to believe and exercise faith in Christ without first knowing sorrow for their sin. They seek to satisfy self and their needs without first seeking to satisfy the needs of salvation, which begins with repentance. Consequently, they appeal for help to obtain freedom from habits, thought patterns and inordinate affections. Knowing something is wrong, they want victory over the plaguing problems but are not able to find relief.

Steps to Growth

How can men grow?

First, we need to understand the difference between our works of the flesh and Satan's deception, temptation and accusation. Satan may tempt us, but we don't sin until we are drawn away ~~of~~ by our own lusts.[10] Satan does not have the power to make us sin. The power lies in ourselves, so before we deal ruthlessly with him, we must deal ruthlessly with ourselves. That's why the Bible says first to submit to God, then to resist the enemy.[11]

What is submitted to grows stronger. What is resisted grows weaker. True liberty is born of submission.

Second, we reckon ourselves dead to the flesh, resist the devil and live righteously in this present evil world.[12]

Third, we don't resist the flesh and reckon the devil dead. Many are fighting the flesh and trying to die to the devil. That's a perversion of both truth and life. You don't get rid of the works of the flesh by warring against Satan but by mortifying the members of your body ... reckoning yourself dead to sin.[13] Godly sorrow and genuine repentance are the method.

The works of the flesh are those deeds, thoughts and motives done in the body without the control of (or out from under the influence of) the Holy Spirit of God. They are natural to the old, unredeemed, carnal nature. The works of the flesh fall naturally into categories: (1) sins of sensual passion: adultery, fornication, uncleanness, lasciviousness; (2) sins of superstition: idolatry and witchcraft (sorcery); (3) sins of social disorder: hatred, variance, emulations, wrath, strife, seditions, heresies, envying and murder; (4) sins of excess: drunkenness and revellings.[14]

Fourth, dying daily is the rule.[15] Death is in the decision. In the conflict between flesh and Spirit, when you decide for the Spirit, you deny (die to) the flesh. Just as resurrection follows death in Christ, so power flows from obedience to God's Word and Spirit.

Fifth, some who have never conquered addictions (the Bible calls them besetting sins[16]) think they are battling Satan when, in reality, they are contending with their own habits and proclivities.

Sixth, sin can go out of the life only by way of the mouth. Repentance precedes faith. Confession without commitment, however, is just vain babbling.[17]

"Gender blender," "lukewarm" and "mixed-up" are but some of the adjectives describing society today. It's imperative, as never before, to hear God's warning. "I am the Lord ... Thou shalt not let thy cattle gender with a diverse kind: thou shall not sow thy field with mingled seed: neither shall a garment mingled of linen and woolen come upon thee."[18] Don't breed a cow with a horse; don't mix iron and clay; don't join Christian faith with heathen belief; don't mix world system-based psychology with biblical theology; don't mingle truth with error.

Lukewarmness is a mixture of hot and cold. It's the character-istic of our day when everything is being mixed together and people no longer acknowledge right and wrong, true and false, black and white. All is compromised to "blend." The gender-blender society. The lukewarm church. But blend makes bland, useless, fit for chaff, holy hogwash and religious refuse. God said He would "spew" it out of His mouth.[19] It nauseates him. Refuse to grow up, and you'll be thrown up.

Men need to know the truth. *Sermons don't set you free; God's truth does.*

Being right doesn't always make you popular, and being pop-ular doesn't always make you right. Christ wasn't popular. He was righteous. He isn't popular today—except with the righteous.

Righteousness issues forth from Calvary. Repentance is the pivotal point between rebellion and reconciliation, which leads to righteousness. Jesus didn't provide us with self-help formulas but with an old wooden cross. That's the dividing line in our world. Not black-white, rich-poor, have-have not, but the cross. That's the issue.

"There is ... no condemnation to them ... who walk not after the flesh, but after the Spirit."[20] The Bible doesn't say, "There is no condemnation" with a period at the end. The qualification for liv-ing without condemnation is walking in the Spirit.

Gaining by Losing

The principle of gain through loss is established by the cross. If you lose your life, you'll save it; if you seek to save it, you'll lose it. Death comes before the resurrection. *There is no resurrection without death and no death in Christ without a resurrection.*

Scripture teaches us that humility precedes blessing.[21]

Jesus taught that true joy is born out of sorrow.[22] Subtraction came before multiplication in the first church. Paul, the apostle, counted all things as loss that he might gain Christ.[23] The Lord said, "Give, and it shall be given."[24] In all these, we lose before we gain.

"You gain by trading" is the message in the parable of the pounds and talents. Trading is a process of exchange, which is the process of life. To gain, we trade the lesser for the greater. Bring your sins to Calvary, and exchange them for the unique plan for which God created you and only He can accomplish.

But dying isn't easy. Surrender doesn't come naturally. Humility is hard on our pride. Losing ourselves, admitting we don't know everything, is no fun. It's better than compromise, however. The nation of Israel compromised with their lusts when Jehovah God was trying to bring them into their promised land. Their feet took them to Canaan, but their hearts kept going back to Egypt. It was easier to give in than to hold out. The softness of their lives resulted from the hardness of their hearts.

The softness in Israel was seen more and more in:

- unwillingness to face hardship
- inability to discipline self
- resistance to reproof and correction
- refusal to face reality
- acceptance of standards of the world around them
- desire for fleshly gratification

Out of the entire nation of Israel, only two men had the faith of God to enter Canaan. They opposed the prevailing opinion of their people. It wasn't easy, but they stood their ground. A generation died in that wilderness; two lived through it. Joshua and Caleb inherited the land and led a new generation. Indefatigable in strength, untiring in effort, relentless in their pursuit of God's promise, they became God's heroes of faith—strong men in tough times.

Have enough guts to die to the flesh. Be willing to fight the forces of evil internally and externally. Determine not to compromise. Make the cross your glory—not your own achievements.

Daniel prophesied, "But the people that do know their God shall be strong, and do exploits."[25]

When all around you people want to take the easy road, are you willing to go by way of the cross? Is there enough godly character in your life to purpose to know God? If so, then in the days that stretch before us, you will be one of those whom God can point to as His workmanship. He will help you to do His will and cause you to work exploits of faith such as the world has never seen.

It's your day!

End Thoughts

- Life is lived on levels and arrived at in stages.
- Success in life is not the aim of the cross; it's the result of the cross.
- What is submitted to grows stronger; what is resisted grows weaker.
- Sermons don't set you free; truth does.
- Being right doesn't always make you popular, and being popular doesn't always make you right.
- Repentance is the pivotal point between rebellion and reconciliation, which leads to righteousness.
- There is no death in Christ without resurrection.
- Humility precedes blessing.
- Softness of life stems from hardness of heart.

Reflections

1. Have you ever struggled over admitting you were wrong? Did things work out worse or better than you expected?
2. What did repentance for sin accomplish in Apostle Paul?
3. Is it easier for you daily to submit to God, die to the flesh or resist the devil?

SIX

THE GREAT RIP-OFF

The men in the outdoor stadium numbered twenty-two thousand strong. They cheered, clapped, shouted and slapped each other on the back with wild enthusiasm. They laughed, cried and even sang together like no sports, military or political crowd I'd ever seen. This was not a riot, not a sporting event, not a review of some country's fighting men. It was a gathering of Christians, and the occasion was a celebration of their manhood under the Lordship of Jesus Christ.

As I prepared to address them, I shivered a little inside. Would my words be adequate? I wondered if any of them had even heard my name before, read my books, heard the teaching to men that we started over a decade ago. If not, how could I sum up thirteen years of men's teaching into one short hour? What one major theme did the Lord want to get across above any others? I had settled on the subject Coach Bill McCartney had heard me teach years before.

Looking out over that football stadium on a midsummer's day, I started them off like I do most of my men's meetings, slapping high-fives and forcefully greeting others with, "Thank God, you're a man!" As I watched them, smiling, pumping hands and sharing the joy of being men, I could not help but swell with admiration for Coach McCartney and his courage and faith in organizing such an event. He was living out his goal to awaken men to the need of being men of their word.

Bill has some similar characteristics to Daniel's. They are both strong. One measure of strength is toughness. Being tough is not being hard. It's the willingness to face reality, a confrontation with truth, and embrace it at the expense of self. Bill's toughness enabled him to endure a grueling football season amidst personal tragedy and a team that made national headlines for both good and bad reasons. Yet he came out on top, number one in the country. No wonder he has something to say to other men.

Being tough is being resilient, durable, even pliable.

My part in Promise Keepers that year was the Saturday morning meeting. The men were enthusiastic and excited, ready for the day. My heart pounded as they took their seats, and I gave them the words I felt God had inspired me to share. It's difficult to summarize a lifetime of lessons, but if you're going to stand strong in the tough times ahead, you need to know a few of the basics of manhood. Just as I gave them to those men that day, I lay them out for you here.

A major sign of manhood is in a man's word. To be conformed to the "image of Christ,"[1] our words must conform to God's Word. God's Word is tough. It outlasts tough times.

Five Propositions Concerning God's Word

Here are five truths concerning His Word:

1. God's Word is His bond.

When God made a promise to Abraham, because He could swear by nothing greater, He swore by Himself.[2] In the new covenant established long after Abraham, in which Christ is the Mediator, Christ Himself is the Word that confirms the promise of salvation.

2. God's Word is the expression of His nature.

Jesus Christ came to earth as the "express image" of the person of God.[3] He told Philip, "Anyone who has seen me has seen the Father!"[4]

One Scripture verse states, "In the beginning was the Word, and the Word was with God, and the Word was God."[5] Christ is the living Word of God.[6] Because God's Word is the expression of His nature, when Christ came, it was necessary that He be the "Word made flesh."[7] The very nature of God is revealed in Jesus Christ. Likewise, Jesus is revealed in the written Word. As Jesus is God's Word revealed, so the Bible is God's Word revealed to us. The Word is made alive in our hearts by the Holy Spirit.

3. God's Word is the measure of His character.

When Jesus Christ referred to Himself as the Alpha and Omega, He was using the first and last letters of the Greek alphabet.[8] In other words, He is the beginning and the end. If he were using the English alphabet, He would say, "I am the A and Z," the first and last. The use of the alphabet is a divine way of revealing the measure of His character.

Think how many times the twenty-six letters in the English alphabet have been used, in words spoken and written, since its inception. Yet it is still as new as the day it was invented. The words may have changed in meaning, spelling or writing, but the alphabet itself is undiminished, interminable and immeasurable. So, too, is Christ.

Think of all the sermons that have been preached from the Word of God; all the revelation from the Word that is known; the books written concerning it; how much it's being used today and yet, it is still as new as the day it was given. There is no end to God's character and, thus, no end to His Word. No matter how much of Himself He reveals, even in eternity, there will be no end to the revelation of His character. The measure of God's character is in His Word.

4. God's Word is magnified above His Name.

God's Name is as good as His Word. If His Word is no good, His Name is no good.

Faith comes by hearing and hearing by the Word of God, the Bible says.[9] The prayer of faith is always made on the basis of His Word. The use of His Name is predicated on His Word. When Jesus said to use His Name, He was literally telling us to use His authority.[10] But the use of His Name comes from the authority of His Word.

5. God's Word is the sole source of faith and the absolute rule of conduct.

"There is none other name under heaven given among men, whereby we must be saved" other than the Name of Jesus Christ.[11] God's Word alone, accepted by faith, has the power of salvation. We are saved by the incorruptible seed of the Word of God. "Man shall not live by bread alone, but by every word ... of God."[12] God's Word stands sure.

History has a way of repeating itself, and though culture may change, the nature of man remains the same. We live in a day not unlike the time of Isaiah the "prince of the prophets." At one time, he prophesied to his generation and nation that their transgressions were not unknown to them.[13] The sins that testified against them were in "transgressing and lying against the Lord, and departing away from [their] God, speaking oppression and revolt, conceiving and uttering from the heart words of falsehood."[14] Isaiah said that "judgment is turned away backward, and justice standeth afar off."[15]

Men familiar with the standard of God's Word know the sins of their countries, how people have mistreated one another and rebelled against authority in cities and homes. For me, in the United States, it seems, at times, that judgment is turned backward, and our system of jurisprudence is more concerned about the rights of criminals than those of victims. Justice seems to "stand afar off" in that it's hard for the common man to find it, yet it appears that certain men can buy it.

Isaiah, speaking by the Spirit of God, said the reason for our ills is because truth is "fallen in the street ... Yea, truth faileth."[16]

Last year, as I prepared for my first ministry trip to a part of the world that was newly liberated from communism, I talked with a gentleman of that nation. "I feel impressed," I told him, "that I should minister on God's Word and on man's word and how important it is to be men of our word and lovers of truth."

"In my country," he said slowly, with a kind but sad expression, "you will first have to teach us what truth is. My people no longer know."

In the aftermath of the collapse of communism, people of his nation came to the terrible realization that their leaders had been lying to them for years. In the trauma of learning of the lies and trying to find the truth, many citizens openly preferred to go back to the way things were. At least then they could believe something in ignorance. Discovering truth, for them, was as hard as digging for gold and silver. They did not know what to believe, and rather than try to discover what was true, they were willing to be content with a lie.

A recent *Time* magazine cover article entitled "Lying" featured the endemic plague we have in the national character of the United States. The writer advanced a premise that "everyone does it." Because of its prevalence, it was being viewed as the norm rather than the exception. A letter to the editor later scolded them with, "I can think of no better way to encourage lying than to tell people that 'everyone's doing it.'"[17]

The truths of God's Word and the overwhelming absence of truth in the world today has tremendous relevance to the way men live their lives. In the book of Genesis, God's Word recounts the creation of man and definitively states Adam was created in the image of God and in His moral likeness.[18] God invested Himself in Adam. In that divine bestowment, God endowed man with creative power, in his loins and in his mouth.

That humanity is able to reproduce a creation in the image of God is one of the greatest wonders of the universe. What is formed in the womb is a creation that is like unto Almighty God. To make the womb the tomb, to destroy what God ordained to be in His image, is sacrilege done to God Himself.

Creative power is also in the power of man's word. Man speaks into existence things and matters that have never existed before in the history of the universe. Incredibly, Scripture says the tongue has the power of life and death.[19] Therefore, words must be spoken in the fear of the Lord. Scripture states we will have to account for every idle word.[20]

Five Propositions Concerning Our Word

Because we are created in the image of God, whatever God's Word is to Him, our word is to be to us. God watches over His Word to perform it. So should we. The same truths relative to God's Word apply to our word.

1. Our word is our bond.

I remember a time in my youth when the character of men was much stronger and richer in integrity than it seems to be now. The moral climate was such that lying, cheating and stealing were gross sins. Those caught in them were dismissed from school, barred from practicing law, voted out of public office and ruined in reputation. When a man gave you his word and shook your hand as the seal, it was better than a signed contract. Often no contract was necessary—a man's word was his bond. In giving his word, a man made a covenant, and the handshake was a sign of that covenant.

Such is not the rule of life today. Lawyers draw up legal papers with infinite pains to cover every detail of the agreement. Yet the paper is only as good as the character of the persons who sign it. Even in marriage, men still vow to remain wed "until death do us part," but too often treat their vow as part of a ritual without any true meaning. In most cases outside of the Christian church, that phrase is eliminated. I even heard one pastor say, "Why make them lie at their wedding?"

Where men do not hold to a high value of truth, they do not place a high value upon their word.

2. Our word is the expression of our nature.

In the early days of my Christian experience and fellowship, we were taught to "sanctify our speech." *Gosh* and *darn* were considered euphemisms for *God* and *damn*. Such minced oaths we conscientiously removed from our vocabularies. So concerned were we with our word that we regularly practiced using King James English. When Nancy and I traveled with our children through Nevada, we joked that we wouldn't even say Hoover Dam but instead, "Hoover Water-stopper."

Salvation was, to us, a total experience. Inside and out, the Holy Spirit was at work to cleanse us from all unrighteousness. A person's words reveal the nature within.

My opinion, which I won't try to justify with chapter and verse of the Bible, is that on the day of God's judgment, movie producers are going to be held personally responsible for what they have done to the world's moral climate by their frequent use of the vilest profanity. Though they deny culpability by saying it is everyday language, they have polluted the minds, hearts and mouths of the world's youth. In my estimation, they are guilty of lowering the standards and literally destroying a generation's culture in their lust for money.

The world uses the Name of Christ profanely in their swearing, while Christians swear by His Name. A man who uses the Name of Jesus as an epithet in everyday conversation cannot be truthful on Sunday in worshipping that Name. The idea of purging our language may need to be revived.

3. Our word is the measure of our character.

The honesty of a man's heart, the depth of manly character, is shown by how he keeps his word. It's called integrity. The prophet, Job, cried out in his deepest need, "I will not remove mine integrity from me."[21]

God commended Job to Satan, saying, "He holdeth fast his integrity."[22]

Job's wife, in exasperation after all his possessions were gone, cried out against him, "Do you still retain your integrity? Why don't you curse God and die?"

Yet the tests Job underwent are not foreign to the tough days we are entering. It's tough when ...

- your wife and children are killed in an auto accident by a drunk.
- your possessions are swept away by a flood or earthquake, and insurance doesn't cover the loss.
- the country of your birth confiscates your property, threatens your family, tortures you and expatriates you to rebuild your life elsewhere.
- a crippling disease takes your eyes just when you launch your career as an artist.

I know men in all these situations. Their integrity upholds them in spite of their losses.

Men who have proved their integrity are held in admiration and great respect. As Scripture says, a man with integrity is one who swears "to his own hurt" and changes not.[23] In other words, he's the kind of man who keeps his word even if it costs him.

4. Our word is magnified above our name.

Our name is only as good as our word. If our word is no good, our name is no good.

Men who do not value their word diminish their personal worth. An amazing number of people submit false resumes for professional positions. Men exaggerate and women lie; then when they are discovered, they fight because they are dismissed or fired. Regardless of the level of their work, their value drops sharply when they are deemed untrustworthy.

5. Our word is the source of faith and rule of conduct for those to whom we give it.

God is a maximizer of men; Satan is a usurper. Christ is Truth; Satan is the father of lies.[24] Satan has the character of a thief who steals, kills and destroys.[25] Satan attacks God's Word in order to lure men into sin. If he attacks God's Word, it's obvious he will attack man's word as well to lure into sin the man and those to whom he gives his word.

When Satan approached Eve in the Garden of Eden, his accusation against God's Word seditiously undermined her faith. Adam eventually denied God's right of possession, rejected His sovereignty and was expelled from the presence of God. By attacking God's Word, Satan stole Adam and Eve's faith, killed their relationship with God and destroyed their lives. His attacks on men's lives today still start with God's Word.

Moses' life was one of confrontation in which he had to withstand privation, ostracization, sedition, idolatry, obdurateness and outright rebellion. He is described as the meekest of men, but like Christ, his meekness was not weakness.[26]

When Moses told Pharaoh that God said to let His people go, Pharaoh rejected his words and accused Moses of trying to blackmail him to make life easier on the Israelites. After the plagues, Pharaoh finally relented, but then he decided to pursue Israel to recover the goods taken from his nation. More than that, Pharaoh attacked God's Word that said, "Let my people go."[27]

The prophet, Elijah, was threatened by Jezebel after he defeated her priests and removed her idol to Baal. The "spirit of the spoiler" in Jezebel did not want God's Word to prevail at the expense of hers. The false prophetess led her people into idolatry, teaching them "deeper truths," which led to immorality and then into Baal worship.

Centuries later, the apostle, Paul, admonished us not to be partakers with those who will not abide in the doctrine of Christ.[28] Satan's subtlety is to attack God's Word and promise us "true" liberty while putting us in bondage. *All sin promises to serve and please but only desires to enslave and dominate.*

In His parable of the sower and the seed, Jesus told us that immediately after the word is sown, Satan comes to steal it.[29] Immediately after conversion comes the temptation to deny the reality of the experience. People discount it, relatives mock it, the desire for old habits increases, and, if we do not stay close to the Lord, God's Word can be stolen, our faith killed, our relationship with God destroyed. But overcoming the attack on God's Word by reading and speaking it concentrates and confirms the relationship with Him.

All sin promises to serve and please but only desires to enslave and dominate.

Satan not only tries to "rip-off" God's Word, but he tries to steal our word as well. Think of a father who promises to take his son fishing. The son immediately prepares, putting the tackle box and fishing pole under his bed while he dreams of the day. Then the night before their fishing trip, the father's friend calls with tickets to a football game, and the father accepts his offer.

Early the next morning, the son is up, eager to get going, only to be told his dad is going to the game instead. Disappointed, the son sulks and refuses to come to dinner that day until threatened. Days of resentful attitude follow until, in exasperation, the father tells the son to change or be punished. The boy's disappointment turns to resentment, then deepens into rebellion. Without realizing his own culpability, the father repeats his behavior and helplessly watches the hardening of his son's heart.

What about the man who constantly promises his wife that he will change but reneges or that he will give her things or take her places but never does? Little does he realize that he is teaching her not to trust his word. Trust is extended to the limit of truth and no more.

Confronting Truth

When I was finished speaking that Saturday morning and was milling around to enjoy the rest of the conference, a man stopped me. He locked his eyes on me and said, "In all my life, I never had a man talk to me the way you did."

"I apologize if I was too hard or if the truth offended you," I began.

"Not that!" he interrupted. "You told me what was wrong with my life. I have been a preacher all my life. Today my wife won't go to church with me, my children have turned their backs on God, and my congregation is smaller than ever. I have been blaming my family, thinking their absence was influencing the members, causing them to leave. But you told me something I have never heard before. You told me it was *my* fault."

"Well–," I started, trying to soothe the intensity of the man's feeling.

"I sat there listening," he said, cutting me off again. "And I heard the truth that my word was my bond, the source of faith to people who listen to me, and that my name is only as good as my word. For the first time in my life, I know what I did to my family.

"All my life, I made promises of what I would do for them, knowing that, even when I said it, with my limited salary and time, I probably couldn't do it. I gave myself credit for the promises and intentions. To me, I was a man with good intentions who wanted to be able to care for my family. I realize now that, to my family, I was a liar.

"All my life I considered myself to be a man of God's Word. Now, all of a sudden, I cannot, in honesty, say that, because I am not a man of my word. If I were a man of God's Word, I would be a man of my word."

With increasing intensity, he finished his message to me like one would pronounce a benediction: "You have just unraveled my whole life. Now I've got to go home and try to put it all together again. I don't know if I can do it, or if they will believe me, but I have to try."

Without waiting for a reply, he turned and walked out of my life. If he reads this, I hope he'll write me. I want to know how it turned out.

Tough? Yeah, that's tough. But real? You bet!

I've listened to men who even give God their word then fail to keep it. They do not realize their word is being ripped off. Their enemy is their own shallow character that doesn't have enough strength in it and also satanic conspiracy to steal their words, kill their influence and destroy their success and their relationships.

The prophet always precedes the deliverer in the scriptural pattern. It's the prophet's role to bring the fear of the Lord upon the hearts of the people, to show them their need of change. As I travel the world and hear people pray for revival, I wonder how a renewing can come when there is no fear of the Lord upon men's hearts to command them to be men of God's Word, shown by being men of their word.

No wonder God is raising up men across the width and breadth of the earth to call men to repent![30] It is time to put away lying and to "speak every man truth" with God and his neighbor.[31] Reverence for God's Word means reverence for *your* word. You were created in the image of God. Be a man of God's Word. Be a man of your own word!

End Thoughts

- God's Word is His bond.
- As God's Word is to Him, our word is to be to us.
- Your name is only as good as your word.
- Your word is the source of faith and rule of conduct for those to whom you give it.
- All sin promises to serve and please but only desires to enslave and dominate.
- Trust is extended to the limit of truth and no more.
- The prophet precedes the deliverer.

Reflections

1. Whose word do you trust more than any other person's?
2. If you were one of the twelve disciples and caught Jesus in a lie, what would it have done to your belief in Him?
3. Have you ever received a "word" from God that later was ripped off? Has your word been ripped off? What can you do this week to help others believe your word?

SEVEN

THE GREATEST GIFT

The restaurant where we sat was lit by glowing sunlight, showering us through massive picture windows. The delicious food matched the cheery ambiance, and my friend's delightful conversation completed the exquisite lunchtime. As our conversation warmed, he confided in me a deeply troubling problem.

"I'm having a problem, or actually a close friend is," he said. "Tom has worked for me for so long, that he's almost like a brother to me. Actually, I'm closer to him than I am to my real brother. We trust him so completely that Jan and I take vacations, leaving the company with him and our kids with his wife. We even spend Christmases together with his family. He's always been a strong Christian, too.

"The other afternoon, Tom came into my office and announced he had just spent his lunch hour meeting with a divorce lawyer," my friend said. "He told me it was set in concrete, so I shouldn't bother trying to talk him out of it.

"Ed, he and his wife have had their share of problems, but they have always managed to work them out. Sure, she's demanding, but they've gone to counseling, and it seemed like both had made compromises for the sake of staying together. Now he says it's over, and the reason he gave me was that he just couldn't forgive her anymore."

His words cast a pall on the warm conversation and reduced us both to somber reflection. I realized that, more than anything, he was experiencing a kind of grief–grief for Tom's wife, for Tom in his error and for the trust he had in Tom that would never again be the same. Tom decided he could not forgive, perhaps not fully realizing he himself had been forgiven by God.

Forgiveness is basic to Christlikeness. God's love is tough enough to continue forgiving, continue loving, regardless of the injustices we do to Him.

Daniel forgave. Even in the face of cruel injustice, he forgave his captors, the men who ransacked and pillaged his native land. He served the very men he had "every right" to hate. Through serving them, he became qualified to lead them. It was tough, but he was stronger because of his forgiveness.

Tough is when:

- you discover your wife is buying other men gifts on your credit card.
- your wife is having an affair with another woman.
- you find out your child is a drug addict.
- you return from vacation and discover you are penniless, in debt, and the partner who put you there while you were gone has left town.
- the church board fires you because you won't perform the ceremony for the chairman's daughter, who is marrying for a third time.
- your stepchildren reject you.
- police lie about your offense to protect themselves.
- your family is hungry, and you can't get work.
- the man who murders your father gets off without prosecution.

I know men who have weathered these circumstances. In every instance, they were forced to choose whether to forgive or not. They all forgave.

God's greatest gift to us is the forgiveness of our sins through Jesus Christ. Jesus promised to send a Comforter who would testify of Him.[1] The testimony of Jesus is that He came into the world to save sinners, of whom you and I, like Paul, the apostle, are chief. His testimony is that while we were yet sinners, Jesus died for us. He did not condemn us but saved us instead. He went to the cross for our offenses and was raised for our justification.[2]

Jesus could have come to earth, preached the Gospel and lived a sinless life. But without earning our forgiveness on that "old rugged cross," Heaven might never have been opened to us. Forgiveness opens; unforgiveness closes. The whole world lies guilty before God and in need of forgiveness for its sin. God's gift to the world is Jesus and His forgiveness, which brings us into right standing before God.

As Christ has forgiven us, He exhorts us emphatically to forgive others. So strong is this principle, that Jesus said if we don't forgive others, God will not forgive us.[3]

When men experience tough times, the only way they can forgive as God forgives is by the power of His Holy Spirit. We do not have the ability in our natural selves. It has to be a supernatural power from the Holy Spirit.

Forgiveness is an expression of true holiness. God is holy. The essence of holiness is love; of love, grace; of grace, mercy; of mercy, forgiveness.

Godly Forgiveness

Over the years, I have been places where men thought holiness was found in outward accoutrements, such as lack of adornment, absence of refinement, legal duty to God, conformity to dress codes—and built barriers between themselves and those who didn't comply with their standards. Most such people aren't toughened against the evil of the world, only hardened, legalistic, unforgiving. Theirs is a call for subjection, not submission.

Forgiveness is always by grace. It's never earned. If forgiveness were earned, we could earn forgiveness for sins. But how could one ever do enough to pay back God for His Son? His forgiveness is impossible to buy. Some mistakenly think their piety, devotion or contributions earn them a place in God's Kingdom. They may find a place in a religious man's kingdom, but not God's.

Carl lived on the east coast and Jim on the West. They were both married, and each had committed adultery. They did not know each other, but I knew each of them. Both of them had confessed their infidelity to their wives, repented and asked forgiveness, but the results were different.

When Jim and his wife dealt with it, she was quick to say she forgave him. However, on occasions when they would differ or quarrel, she would remind him of his affair. It was her "trump card" in the game of marriage. It was also leverage in their times of intimacy.

It took some time, effort, prayer and a whole lot of talking before Carl's wife said she forgave him. Once she forgave him, she never brought it up again. When he told me what had happened, how the marriage had been healed, Carl said the marriage "is stronger now than ever." When God forgives us, He remembers our sins no more, though the devil certainly does.[4] You can keep other people in bondage—as well as yourself—by remembering past offenses.[5]

If a man borrows twenty dollars from me with the promise to pay it back the next time I see him, what's the first thing I think of when I see him again? My twenty dollars. If he doesn't repay me, then every time I see him, the first thing I will think of is the money he owes me. It will always be between us. For the obstacle to be removed, either I must forgive him or he must pay me the debt. Restitution follows, not precedes, forgiveness.

And if I'm to forgive without his repayment, I must do it by grace. Once you've been forgiven, freely forgive. Our forgiveness of others is our greatest gift to them. Forgiveness cannot demand works or payment before being given. Then it would be earned and no more of grace.

Men who have sinned and asked God to forgive them but don't forgive themselves build a barrier between themselves and God. In not forgiving even when God has, they make themselves greater than God. It is a terrible error to continue chastising yourself when God's forgiveness is so freely given.

Genuine Forgiveness

When forgiveness is given, it must be offered in the same spirit in which it was asked. When a sincere person wants to clear himself of a wrong attitude, error in judgment or misperception and asks to be forgiven, for the one forgiving to pass it off flippantly insults the other's integrity.

A man approached me during the break in one of our Christian Men's Events and asked if he could see me afterward. I had a plane to catch, but I promised I'd make a brief meeting possible. Promptly after the meeting, he met me backstage.

"Mr. Cole," he said, "I saw you a couple of years ago, and I really didn't like you. I thought you were arrogant, bombastic and unloving. Actually, what I thought of you was a bad word, but I won't repeat it to you now. Someone convinced me to come with him today, and I realized I'd been wrong. You talk tough, but it is a toughness in love, not a hardness of heart. I wanted to be sure I saw you today to ask you to forgive me for my attitude."

Now this man's attitude never hurt me or touched me in any way. I've lived with critics for so long that I could easily have brushed him off and said, "Don't worry about it." But for me to treat him offhandedly or tell him he didn't need to ask forgiveness would have been to minimize his sincerity. So I faced him squarely and shook his hand. "Thank you, sir, for telling me that," I said. "I appreciate your honesty, and I forgive you. Let's pray."

He left without a bothersome conscience. I left without a lowered esteem for him. The forgiveness was given in the same spirit in which it was asked, and the episode was over.

Forgiveness is always in spirit, not just word. Saying you forgive (or making an effort to show it) when it is not genuinely in your spirit does not complete it. God's forgiveness is given to us not only in His Word, where He tells us He has forgiven us, or on Calvary, where He accomplished it, but in sending His Spirit into our spirits to witness that the act of forgiveness has been completed.

A famous football coach left his office for the practice before the year's big game. Just before he left, his wife had asked him a question about their sons, who were misbehaving. He had snapped at her and told her to deal with it, didn't she know he was getting ready for the "big game"? On the way to the stadium, however, he realized the game was only for the day, but he would have his sons for life. So he pulled off the crowded freeway, knowing it would make him late, and called the house. He spoke to each of his children, then to his wife.

"Look, I'm sorry," he said. And he proceeded to solve the problem that created the tension in the first place.

His wife hadn't had a quiet moment as he'd had on the freeway. His call was unexpected and took her off guard. She had been dealing with upset children, her own emotions and the problems he solved by phone, and she hadn't had time to compose herself. Without really meaning it, she said, "I forgive you." But her forgiveness was only in word, not in spirit.

That evening, when the coach came home, the situation was altogether different. His wife had spent time thinking about how great it was that he had called. She thought lovingly of him and had forgiven him deeply. Forgiveness had been consummated.

Forgiveness must be completed. God's forgiveness is ours. But we do not receive it until we ask for it. Though He has forgiven us, it is consummated only by our receiving it. Acknowledging what Christ has done is not the end of forgiveness. Receiving His forgiveness results in peace and joy that know no equal.

Extraordinary Forgiveness

Forgiveness can come from the most extraordinary sources and result in the most extraordinary circumstances. A man named

Al, whom I met in Phoenix, told me the incredible story of how his life changed. By his own admission, he was a "ragin' Cajun" from the bayou country around New Orleans. Drinking, cussing and fighting were part of his lifestyle. Going to jail when drunk was a way of life.

But Al's wife wanted a better existence for herself and their two girls. Each Sunday, the bus would take the girls to the church. Two sweet little Christian ladies visited the house periodically to talk with his wife and make sure the girls would be in Sunday School. He was usually able to avoid their visits, but when they caught him unexpectedly, he cursed them, hurling as much verbal abuse as possible to scare them off.

Then one day his wife packed herself and her children and left the house. Al was free, with no family to inhibit his wild ways any longer.

One Saturday night after his wife left, his friend and their dates were waiting downstairs for a night on the town when the doorbell rang. The friend answered it and ran upstairs to tell Al, "Two funny-looking women are downstairs."

In an instant, Al guessed who they were and felt his anger rise.

"Tell them to get out of here," Al said.

Soon his friend returned to Al's room. "Man, they won't go!" the friend said. "Me and the girls are getting out of here. This is weird!"

Al ran downstairs in a rage and saw the two prim, elderly women seated on his couch with their hands folded on their laps. He greeted them with cursing, threatening that if they ever set foot on his property again, he would bash in their faces. He hurled one vulgarity after another at them. Inside, though, he was trembling, not from anger, but from fear of these two serene spirits sitting before him.

When he finally took a breath, one spoke up confidently. "We know all about you," she said. "You don't scare us. We're here because we want you to know the Lord forgives you, and we do, too. We believe the Lord sent us here so you could be saved."

It's one thing to pray for an answer, another to be an answer.

That sent Al into another tirade. He told me he was never so scared in all his life as he was while cussing at those ladies. Again he paused, and they took their opportunity.

"We know you want us to leave, but while we were praying, the Lord told us to come here because He wants to save you."

Those two little ladies were stronger in spirit than Al. No matter what he said, they sat like immoveable granite statues on his living room couch, unwilling to surrender their territory. Finally, Al ran out of words to say, sat down in a chair and began to weep. By the end of the evening, he had surrendered his life to his new-found Savior.

"Man, they were tough on me," Al said. "They were strong. But they won me to Christ."

Those ladies had God's forgiveness for Al in their hearts. All Al had to do was receive it. It was no use to him until he did so. *It's one thing to pray for an answer, another to be an answer.* Forgiving people can become God's answer to another's prayers.

To forgive as God forgives can come only by the power of His Spirit. Where His Holy Spirit ushers in forgiveness, release follows.

At one of our men's meetings in Anaheim, California, a man stood up to make a confession. "Tonight I gave my heart to Christ," he said, "and I realize I need to ask my son to forgive me. We need God's help. I haven't been a good father, and it's hurt him. Will you pray for me?"

From the podium where I was standing, I asked him where his son was. He pointed down the row of seats to where the son was sitting. I asked the young man to stand.

"Do you believe your father means what he says?" I asked the teen-man.

"Yes," he answered.

Immediately, his father looked toward him and asked, "Will you forgive me?"

"Yes," his son answered.

The other men parted to allow the father to go to his son. While they embraced, the rest of the men stood to their feet applauding, whistling and slapping high fives.

The month following, I heard what happened after their reconciliation. The father and son went home that evening and told the mother and daughter. What the son and daughter had never known was that their parents had never married. They didn't believe in marriage when they settled down together, and he had continued to resist any suggestion of it through the years.

After the family rejoiced together in their new relationship, they went their ways to retire for the night. In the privacy of their bedroom, the man asked his mate to forgive him for not marrying, and he proposed to her. She agreed. They called their children to the living room again to tell them what was happening and ask the children to forgive them. The following week was filled with excited preparation for their wedding day.

The next Sunday night, at the close of the evening service, the pastor asked the congregation to remain seated for something special. The father and his son walked to the front of the auditorium and stood, looking toward the back as the organ started to play the wedding march. In walked the mother and daughter. The children stood beside their parents, and when the pastor asked, "Who gives this couple to be married," they said in unison, "We do!" Forgiveness had brought both release and unity.

Forgive and be forgiven. It's God's way!

Your greatest gift today is forgiveness, to be imparted or received. In tough times, you can be your own best friend or worst enemy. By forgiveness, you do yourself a service; by unforgiveness, a disservice.

Forgiveness is a mature trait of a manly character. You can open a whole new world for someone, including yourself, by dying to your own feelings and letting God's Spirit work in your life. Try it. You won't just like it–you'll love it. And forgiveness is even better given than received.

End Thoughts

- Forgiveness opens; unforgiveness closes.
- When God forgives us, He remembers our sins against us no more.
- Your forgiveness of others is your greatest gift to them.
- Forgiveness is always in spirit, not just in word.
- It's one thing to pray for an answer, another to be an answer.

Reflections

1. What were you taught about forgiving others as a child?
2. What element of Christ is within you now that can help you forgive others?
3. Is there someone in your life who is the most difficult person for you to forgive? What can you do this week to start forgiving that person?

EIGHT

GRIT, GUTS AND GLORY

"We shall sodomize your sons, emblems of your feeble masculinity, of your shallow dreams and vulgar lies. We shall seduce them in your schools, in your dormitories, in your gymnasiums, in your locker rooms, in your sports arenas, in your seminaries, in your youth groups ... The Family Unit–spawning ground of lies, betrayals, mediocrity, hypocrisy and violence will be abolished .... All churches who condemn us will be closed. Our only gods are handsome, young men."[1]

Homosexual leaders now publicly admit their use of Hitler's Mein Kampf as their blueprint for overtaking American society. Malicious, contemptuous and offensive, they leave us without a question as to the fight we have on our hands to preserve our freedoms and families.

The fabric of the world around us is being torn to pieces. I received this heartbreaking letter a few years ago:

Dear Dr. Cole:
Your book, *Maximized Manhood*, is a very wonderful book. I pray that it gets into the hands of as many non-Christian men as possible as soon as possible. It came too late in my life. I killed my wife in October. Had I had something like this to reach to, my life would have been different. There are so many men and women in desperate need of you.
God bless you.
Joe

The tragic irony about Joe's letter is that it came years after the first publication of *Maximized Manhood*. Who knows the number of Christians around Joe who never shared it or the Bible with him—the ones at work, in the neighborhood or from high school who did not give Joe that which could save his marriage and, very literally, his wife.

We're not playing at life. We're living it. Playing footsy with the devil while the world goes to Hell is a heinous sin of omission. It is immoral. God says, "Knowing what is right to do and then not doing it is sin."[2]

Lower morality leads to higher mortality. It's as true today as ever, whether the cause is immoral cowardice, lewdness or hatred. Promiscuity practiced by men with low moral standards is creating the high mortality rate through abortion and disease. The plague of AIDS in the United States has been spread through homosexual promiscuity.

Crimes by amoral and rabid gang members, drug addicts, hate-filled racists and Mafia members are forcing law-abiding citizens into returning to days when cities were walled and castles were safe fortresses. Walled neighborhoods are commonplace. Barred windows, barricaded doors or security systems are now the norm throughout most of the United States.

Moral courage is needed to live in an immoral world. The greater the immorality, the greater the courage must become. A man needs courage:

- when told to be silent about Jesus or lose his job.
- to decide to work part-time to be available to his two daughters after your wife runs off with another man.
- to tell his wife of his infidelity and ask for her forgiveness.

- to begin another business after the first failed.
- to love those who don't love him.
- to stay in school when his friends drop out.
- to say "no" when most of the class is saying "yes."

Such courageous men, friends of mine, are who I call my "heroes."

Moral versus immoral is the conflict of the ages. Philosophers have theorized the nature of them both; humanitarians have acted upon them; theologians have propounded doctrines of them; politicians have codified propositions concerning them; jurists have endeavored to interpret them; academicians have attempted to define them; but only the Bible gives the truth about them.

Man was made a moral creation, to live under a moral government by a moral law and to be God's moral agent on earth. When man sinned, both he and the world he lives in became immoral. The world system as well as the world itself are now basically immoral and must be converted to become moral.

Morality Personified

The advent of the Lord Jesus Christ into the world was the personification of absolute morality. A lawyer who presumed to know morality asked Jesus what was the greatest commandment in the Law. He was trying to find some flaw in Jesus—personally, philosophically, morally or scripturally. The wisdom of Christ's answer is foundational for the eternal good of all men.

Jesus said unto him, Thou shalt love the Lord thy
God with all thy heart, and with all thy soul, and

with all thy mind. This is the first and great commandment. And the second is like unto it, Thou shalt
love thy neighbour as thyself. On these two commandments hang all the law and the prophets.[3]

Everything that God revealed in the Old Testament, Jesus
summed up in three sentences and two commandments. With that
statement Jesus revealed that the ceremonial, judicial and moral
law given under Moses could be condensed into two commandments. *Jesus' answer to love God and others became the moral law
of love, the substance of all true morality among men.*

Morality was no longer a hard, binding, legalistic application
but a spirit in which grace and truth gave understanding and the
Spirit of God gave guidance. Men birthed into the Kingdom of God
understand that it is a moral government with a moral law; that
the Church is God's moral agency on earth; and that man has a
moral constitution, is God's moral agent in the world and has been
given God's authority to exercise His will on earth. Morality is
imparted when righteousness is imputed to man by faith.

The New Testament writer James dealt with members of the
church who professed the Christian faith but continued in their
old, worldly habits. He blasted them with, "Ye adulterers and adul-
teresses, know ye not that friendship of the world is enmity with
God? Whosoever therefore will be a friend of the world is the
enemy of God."[4] Loving what is immoral while professing to be
moral agents of God is spiritual adultery.

No, we don't live perfect lives. But in a true relationship with
God in Christ, there is a separation between us and the world with
its corruption. When Christians do something immoral, if they are

truly indwelt by the Spirit of God, they repent. They are grieved to have grieved God. When made aware of doing that which is contrary to His will, Christians have a fervent desire to make it right.

The Contradiction of Modern Morals

Today's media and politicians are propagating a terrible contradiction. It is vociferously and viciously advocated by an antichrist spirit. The enigma is in a man's sexuality, or sexual orientation or preference, as they would say.

The Bible is plain when it says that sexual immorality is not to be found among Christians.5 When a prominent Christian leader is found to have committed adultery or homosexuality or has been sexually indiscreet, he is immediately flouted in the media as a hypocrite and taunted as "fallen humanity." A Christian's mistake is not allowed, forgiven or forgotten, even if he is one of those who repents and makes restitution.

On the other hand, homosexuals who call themselves Christians while continuing in their immoral practices are not viewed by the media and legislators as sinners or hypocrites. Instead, they are protected and defended.

Using the same thought process that the homosexuals use to advocate their "righteousness" before God, it would then be all right for Christian heterosexuals to live in adultery if married or live in fornication while single. The media tout civil rights for some but bury moral standards for everyone else.

By the homosexual standard, there is no value to marriage. It is disregarded as an archaic institution and not as a God-given covenant for the benefit of the family unit and the community.

Descending from that premise in the lunacy of today's reasoning brings us to where we are now—with homosexuals who are pedophiles (child molesters) trying to pass laws to legalize the sodomizing of children. Instead of being outraged at such a damnable agenda, the media promote it with little comment. The acronym for their "Man-Boy Love" organization is regularly reported without any mention of its perversion.[6]

"Is the press fair?" Mike Royko asked in a column syndicated in newspapers throughout America. He was reporting on a Chicago columnist who wrote an "open letter" to Chicago Bears football coach Mike Ditka. In the column, the man had attacked Ditka, referring to him with the words *boorish*, *pathetic*, *monster*, *egomaniac*, *psychosis* and *lunatic*. What had Ditka done? He had called the reporters a vulgar name for the stupid questions they had asked him.

Royko went on to say that another story appeared in the same newspaper, less than half as long, buried somewhere inside, concerning a former reporter from the paper who had been indicted the day before on 196 felony counts. What were his crimes? He is accused of using his position at the newspaper "to persuade publicity-hungry, inner-city high school athletes to have sex with him or with prostitutes. He allegedly liked to videotape the young men and the hookers."

Royko's complaint: "It was three brief paragraphs with no comment. No words such as 'monster,' 'pathetic,' 'psychosis.' All of which might lead a reasonable person to ask what is more socially significant: a sports columnist's anger at a football coach's language or the threat of AIDS to some child-athletes who were allegedly exploited by a perverted sportswriter."[7]

The media's "messiah complex" is obviously flawed. Clearly a double standard prevails. But morality cannot be one thing for some and another for others. Do away with the Bible and the resulting "dark ages" would make those of centuries ago look like child's play. Yet there are those who have publicly stated, with the media reporting it, that they think it would be a pleasure to return to those days where they could burn Christians at the stake.

Moral correspondence is the only communication God knows. He hates the hypocrisy in those who love Him "with their lips" while their hearts are far from Him.[8] Men need to be moral in thought, motive, word and deed. Our world needs the morality men give it.

Thought–Father to the Deed

No man becomes immoral in deed without first becoming immoral in thought. There is no seduction without flirtation. Men are seduced to commit adultery with the world after first flirting with it. The illegitimate thought gives birth to the immoral act.

The prophet, Balaam, loved the wages of unrighteousness. He was a true prophet of God. His messages for Israel were God's blessings for the nation. But King Balak tempted him with money and tried to seduce Balaam to prophesy calamity upon Israel. Balaam flirted with the idea until he succumbed. "The eye is the lamp of the body," Christ said in His wisdom.[9]

Balaam looked with longing on Balak's offer. Like Lot's wife, who centuries earlier looked back and became a pillar of salt, Balaam looked for too long. There is a difference between lingering and longing. One is waiting; the other is desiring. The difference is in affection.

Finally, when Balaam was not under God's anointing to prophesy but still coveted the king's gold, he advised Balak to have his women seduce the Israelites and incur God's displeasure. The resulting weakness would allow Balak's army to defeat the Israeli army. God's recompense for Balaam's immorality was a plague in Israel and death by the sword for him.[10]

Daniel maintained his morality under the most trying of times. We have no record that he lied, coveted, cheated, shirked responsibility or betrayed his manhood in any way. He is an example to all men of righteousness in integrity and courage.

Man's moral constitution comprises intellect, discerning between right and wrong; sensibility, which appeals either to right or wrong; and will, which decides the issue. Man's conscience provides knowledge of self in relation to known laws of right and wrong. Reading the Bible doesn't just give knowledge to the intellect and inscribe God's commandments upon the tablets of the heart. It programs the standard for the conscience, which bears witness to behavior.

A defiled conscience provides little restraint against evil doing. One who has a seared conscience (as "with a hot iron"[11]) is no longer sensitive to moral moorings. Nevertheless, like the will, the conscience cannot be destroyed.

My friend, Al, has struggled to reprogram his conscience after years of reckless pursuit of self-gratification. It's worth the struggle. A friend in the same situation learned from God's Word that he was to renew his mind. As a young Christian newly off drugs, he started devouring the Word and listening to tapes of Christian messages from every source he could find. As a result, today he pastors a growing church of five thousand. Conscience judges according to the standard impressed upon it from the knowledge of God, the social standard and the Word of God.

The Ethics of Morality

Jesus commanded the early church to wait for the promise of the Father.[12] He prayed for the Father to send His Spirit to indwell them. They would be able to carry on His ministry by the same Spirit that indwelt Christ and raised Him from the dead. He promised they would become His witnesses in Jerusalem, Judea, Samaria, and to the uttermost parts of the earth.[13] It would have been immoral to have received spiritual gifts and then utilized them only for the benefit of the believers huddled within the four walls of that meeting.

When Jesus was tempted to turn stone into bread, He refused. The temptation He refused was to use for personal advantage what was meant for the good of others. It's called the "lust of the flesh," or coveting for self what is meant for the benefit of others.

Equally immoral is to preach what you don't practice. Some try to practice what they preach. More accurately, *we are to preach what we practice.* I heard a preacher tell his congregation, "Shepherds don't breed sheep, sheep do," meaning it was their task to bring people to church. True, but for him, it was an excuse to tell them to do something he wasn't willing to do himself.

Tommy Barnett pastors a large, thriving church in Arizona. As a young man, he was a renowned evangelist. As a pastor, he was above average. But one day, he realized that if he was to encourage his people to talk to others of Christ's love, he would have to set the example personally. So he disciplined himself to tell someone every day about Jesus Christ. That was the day he became an extraordinary man.

In his daily quest, Pastor Barnett found needy people everywhere, and he and his congregation began to meet those needs. The result was explosive growth to become one of the nation's largest and most imitated churches.

Is it not immoral to do for missions what you won't do at home? I can remember a battle I won and another I lost. Some years ago, the congregation I pastored expanded, and we needed to build a new educational unit. The architect drew up the plans in accordance with traditional Sunday School layouts. The prevailing philosophy at that time was, "Divide and multiply." I disagreed.

My plan was to build a two-floor structure having no small rooms, only one big room on each floor. We would then make rolling partitions for Sundays and use it for other purposes during the week. How did I know I was years ahead of my time? I told everybody I thought (and still think) it immoral to spend all that money on a building to be used only ninety minutes a week. Choosing function over form makes for an architectural success.

The battle I lost was in my last pastorate. The church was on a valuable piece of real estate in town. My advice was to sell it and buy a five-story office building downtown. We would put the church on the fifth floor, offices on the fourth, and rent out the first three. The rent would cover the monthly payments and allow offerings to be used entirely for ministry at home and abroad. The congregation would not think of it, although other pastors since have done similar concepts with great success. It strikes me as immoral to sit on property worth millions and use it to house a congregation four hours a week. A business would go broke the first month with that philosophy.

It is immoral:
- to devote effort on something that is not vital in order to avoid censure or criticism.
- to keep silent when a word is necessary.
- to accept doctrine when knowing it is not scriptural.
- to lower standards just to make yourself acceptable to others.
- to cheat on your income tax.
- to lie to your employer to avoid responsibility for a costly error.

Daniel and his friends were men of great courage. They had to be bold to engage in civil disobedience. They stood to lose position, power, prestige and everything else, including their lives. What kind of courage did the three young men have, while feeling the heat of the fire, to tell the king that to live or die was nothing compared to denying their God? To them, the honor of God meant more than life itself.

"I want the company of the godly ... in the land; they are the true nobility," the psalmist said.[14] "I will make the godly of the land my heroes, and invite them to my home."[15]

It may be tough to program your conscience to become aware of morality and immorality. It's tougher still to stand up to the immorality and keep yourself moral in spite of the pressures. *Yet toughest of all is to live with the unmitigating consequences of immorality.*

We live in tough times, but men of moral strength can still thrive. The darker the night, the brighter the light. You are God's moral agent. Let your light shine.

End Thoughts

- Lower morality leads to higher mortality.
- Moral courage is needed to live in an immoral world.
- To receive the Spirit of God and use it only to benefit the church is immoral.
- It may be tough to live morally and tougher to stand up to immorality, but toughest of all is to live with the consequences of immorality.
- The darker the night, the brighter the light.

Reflections

1. How is lower *morality* leading to higher *mortality* in the world today?
2. What do you think Daniel's standards were in politics? in personal finances? in listening to others? in choosing friends? in working for his boss? What things may have been in his thoughts that are not in your thoughts?
3. What can you do to raise your moral standards and increase your moral courage?

NINE

SCRIPTURAL ILLITERACY

A bumper sticker on the car in front of me had this message: "Illiterate? Write for free help." Amusing or sardonic, it has a bite to it. Illiteracy is a plague to human development; likewise, scriptural illiteracy hinders spiritual development.

A lady wrote my office, asking for advice in regard to her present status in marriage. Both she and her husband attended the same church until he decided not to attend there anymore. He told her the minister did not provide him with the kind of teaching he longed to have. Being involved in many activities, she felt duty-bound to stay where she was.

She went to her pastor for advice, and he agreed she should stay while she let her husband go elsewhere. "He never really was a part of this congregation, and you were," the pastor said.

She wrote to me because her husband had read some of my books, and she thought I could help him since now they were "drifting apart" in the marital relationship. "What shall I do?" she asked. In the quandary and confusion of her writing, she indirectly disclosed that she was not intimately familiar with the Bible. No wonder she could not discern between "good" advice and godly counsel.

She is not alone in her predicament. Innumerable people who name the Name of Christ are suffering from the same malady. They attempt to live a Christian life based upon what people say, advice given, articles read, radio programs listened to and TV programs viewed. When the tough times come, they realize that trying to

"Counselors determine the destiny of kings." build a solid foundation of faith on such ephemeral underpinnings is akin to attempting to build the Empire State Building on the ocean.

Jesus gave us the wisdom of God in the parable about building on a rock or sand.[1] Building on sand may seem safe–until the storm comes. The building is supported by the foundation upon which it is built, not its superstructure. *Building a godly life on the sand of scriptural illiteracy is impossible.* There will be nothing to stand on when tough times come.

"Counselors determine the destiny of kings" is a principle illustrated repeatedly in the Bible and stated more than once in this book.[2] When a man needs counsel, he needs godly counsel, not just good advice. One is divine, the other human. Good advice is based on human wisdom. Godly counsel is based on the wisdom of God's Word.

Here are three great preliminaries to understanding a passage from the Bible.

- Understand it in depth, not by mere acquaintance.
- Understand it in the light of the whole Bible, not as a text by itself.
- Understand it for the purpose of obedience. To the degree you are willing to obey, God will give you understanding.[3]

Know the whole Word and obey it. This takes your whole mind. *A man without an organized system of thought will always be at the mercy of the man who has one.*

We are to love God with all of our minds.[4] In tough days, if we do not diligently apply ourselves to study, we will not survive the whims of doctrine that float through our environment. Those who can organize their presentations to twist and distort reality for evil purposes will be as wolves in sheep's clothing and devour those who have not built their lives around the systematic study of God's Word.

In United States' elections, politicians grossly distorted and misapplied God's Word. Their twisted readings of Scripture are little scrutinized or analyzed by the populace or the media. Only those who contend for truth take exception to the perversion of God's Word.

Wanting to sound religious to get votes is of no consequence to the illiterate, only to the scripturally literate. The politician's only foe is the spiritually attuned, regardless of the immorality of mis-quoting Scriptures to suit one's personal bias.

Columnist Cal Thomas once wrote of this trend: "Why is this important to anyone but theologians and the devout? Because a flawed or a false theology can influence the political direction of a person or a nation. 'As a man thinks in his heart, so is he' Proverbs 23:7. If a candidate or a president and vice-president claim to believe and order their lives according to Scripture, but misinterpret, misunderstand or misapply biblical instructions, disaster can result. The Bible is full of such instances in which leaders did precisely that ... 'For we have made falsehood our refuge and we have concealed ourselves with deception' Isaiah 28:15."[5]

Search for Truth

The study of God's Word is like mining for precious minerals and jewels. It takes effort. The Proverb states you will discover truth when you search for it as for buried treasure.[6] In contrast, little effort is required to obtain good advice, listen to a sermon or watch television.

Daniel was a learned youth and a wise man. *Studious* is not an adjective for non-athletes but is a characteristic of real manhood. Recently, a world-famous golf champion went to an alcohol rehabilitation clinic for his alcoholism. When he returned to the golf circuit, he said he had read a book about Hollywood Henderson's battle with the drug and how he overcame it. The man confessed it was the first book he had read since junior high school. Being literate in literature became a major step in his recovery.

How much more necessary is becoming scripturally literate to those desiring to overcome the world, the flesh and the devil? The Bible is not merely a good source for playing trivia games. It is the very foundation upon which both natural and eternal life rests. Knowledge of God's Word is a bulwark against deception, temptation, accusation and even persecution.

Dan is a pastor friend from Oregon who underwent some trying times in his early years of ministry. After his salvation experience as a teen, he spent years consistently studying the Word and looking forward to the day he would enter the ministry. When his company experienced a financial setback and his job was eliminated, he decided it was a good time to fulfill his desires. With three children at home and a wife who didn't work outside the home, his family felt an immediate financial pinch.

Making a transition from secular work to the ministry is diffi-cult at best. Dan's transition, from a steady paycheck for doing something he understood to depending entirely on the Lord's pro-vision for a work he was just learning, was tough on the whole family. Taking engagements when he could get them, traveling for days away from home, he avidly pursued the care of his family and the ministry. His wife and children stood devoutly beside him, and the times of difficulty passed into a great learning experience that has served him well. With the children grown and gone and the church thriving, he allowed himself some personal reflection with me the last time we were together. His story struck me.

About nine months into the period of his unemployment, his ministry just beginning, a friend invited him to lunch. Excited to see someone with whom he hadn't socialized in a long time, Dan eagerly thumped his friend's back when they met at the restaurant and sat down to enjoy a sumptuous "free" lunch. When the meal was over, Dan's friend grew serious as they drank coffee. "Dan, I wanted to talk to you personally," he said, lowering his voice.

Dan braced himself, knowing only something serious would require this gravity–perhaps a need for counsel or, he hoped, a financial gift to help him through this lean time.

"Dan, I've really prayed about this, and, as a friend, I wanted to tell you that I think you're doing the wrong thing." Seeing that Dan didn't flinch, his friend was emboldened. "You know, my wife says your kids aren't always getting a balanced diet. I know your son attended a father-son school function alone because you weren't there for him. And once while you were gone, your wife's car broke down, and she was stuck trying to handle it alone. It's just not right, Dan."

Dan accepted his friend's counsel at first. The man was an elder in his home church, a brother with whom he'd shared some great times of worship and fellowship. But as he continued to speak, Dan's guilty feeling subsided, and indignation rose up in its place. Dan allowed his friend to continue for a long time without rebuttal, giving himself time to sort through the rush of emotion. Jesus' words, "I was a stranger, and ye took me not in: naked, and ye clothed me not" ran through his mind.[7]

When Dan finally spoke, he tried to do so deliberately and carefully, but his words came out in a rush. "You mean, you saw my children going hungry, and you didn't give them any food?" he asked.

The man set down his coffee cup, and his benevolent look turned to surprise.

"You knew that my son had to go to the father-son event at school alone, and you didn't offer to go with him in my place? You knew about our car breaking down, and you left my wife to deal with the mechanics and inconveniences all alone? But you come to me today as a 'friend'? I value your friendship, but what you're saying to me now is not from a friend. I don't reject you, but I reject what you've said."

Dan went on in ministry. God provided for his family and gave him greater wisdom as he pressed on.

His story simply illustrates that one characteristic we must have in facing tough times is faith in our brothers. But we must be scripturally literate to know who our brother is. Good advice is not godly counsel. Not everyone who says, "Lord, Lord" will enter into the Kingdom of God as one of our brothers in Christ.[8] We must be careful about whose counsel we accept.

When Daniel was thrown into the lions' den, it was the king, not Daniel, who suffered the torment of worry all night. God's care for Daniel did not prevent him from being thrown into the den, but it consisted of the greater miracle of shutting the lions' mouths. God's protective custody was made possible by Daniel's obedience to His Word.

The Lions in Our Lives

There's another application for Daniel's story. Lions are fierce—they are the "kings of the jungle." Their roar is so frightening it literally causes their quarry to freeze with fear, giving the lions opportunity to launch their voracious attack.

Symbolically, the lions in our lives are jealousy, anger, malice, vengeance, greed, strife, spite, drugs and other assorted enemies of well-being. The lions' den is that pit of persecution or dungeon of depression in which we are held at the mercy of such thoughts, emotions and habits that would devour us.

Glen discovered his wife's promiscuity by accident. Though she generally took care of the household accounts, one day, in her absence, he took the checkbook and started paying his bills. Noticing something peculiar with his credit card statement, he called to inquire what the charges were and where they had been made. The shock of discovering his wife was buying gifts for other men was emotionally paralyzing. The lions of anger, jealousy, hatred, revenge and even murder roared in his mind and heart.

Recovering his mental and emotional equilibrium, Glen fell on his face on the floor and cried out to God for help and healing from the deep wound of betrayal. As he lay there under the weight of

God has a strategy to overcome every obstacle.

that great agony, something remarkable happened. The weight came off him, almost in a physical sense. Peace came into his heart, rational thought to his mind and stability to his emotions.

When he confronted his wife after fasting and prayer, she admitted her guilt. In response, he told her, "I love you. You are God's gift to me."

They were still far from the communication necessary to resurrect the marriage, but Glen had already withstood his biggest trial. The mouths of the lions raging against him in the den of his mind and heart were stopped. Figuratively, it was as real to him as it was literally to Daniel.

Glen told me his story later and attributed the change in his life to God. "When I disciplined myself to the Word, my life changed, and what I learned kept me from being destroyed. Since deciding to become a man of God, this is the first sign I've had that I'm really becoming a new person. Before, I would have at least told her to get lost, tried to find the guy and who knows what else. Thank God for His grace."

The Word produced the spirit of a Daniel in him. It was as daring and bold for him to forgive his wife as the heroic acts of men of old. He is one of those Daniel prophesied would "do exploits" because they "do know their God."9

God has a strategy to overcome every obstacle. We find it in His Word. When Naaman, Israel's warrior captain, went to Elisha to be healed of his leprosy, he was incensed at the instructions to go bathe in the River Jordan. He was also insulted that the prophet sent his servant instead of coming himself. What he didn't realize is that without faith, it is impossible to please God.[10] Obedience to God's Word through the prophet was an act of faith, and dipping in the Jordan was the act of humility. *Humility precedes blessing.* God is not impressed by people who think they are important.[11]

For Naaman to insist it was his way or no way would have left him a leper. By humility, faith and obedience, he walked away clean from his "incurable" disease. The glory of God was in the victory over leprosy, but the strategy was in the wisdom of God.

Wisdom Begets Strategy

God's strategies are the product of His wisdom. Satan's strategy is to divide because a divided house cannot stand.[12] God's strategy is to create unity. "Two are better than one ... if one prevail against him, two shall withstand him; and a three-fold cord is not quickly broken."[13] There's strength in unity.

Wisdom produces a strategy. Wisdom is the principal thing, but fools despise it. It gives a long and good life, riches, honor, pleasure and peace. Wisdom's characteristics are from the character of God. Wisdom hates pride, arrogance, corruption, deceit. The fear of the Lord, which is to hate evil, is the beginning of wisdom. To reject the fear of the Lord is to reject knowledge. The beginning of wisdom is to depart from evil.[14] Satan is without the fear of the Lord and has knowledge but not wisdom, so he never knows when to stop. He who has the wisdom of God has power over Satan.

God gives wisdom to those in need. When you need a miracle, pray for wisdom that will give you a strategy. In tough times, you need a strategy:

- to get out of debt.
- to win back your wife's love.
- to succeed in business.
- to raise your children in the ways of God.
- to fill churches.
- to raise funds for church growth.
- to save time, not waste it.

Mining God's Word is how you discover the source of all wisdom. Jesus Christ is made unto us wisdom, righteousness, sanctification and redemption. All the treasures of wisdom are hid in Him.[15]

Boldness—An Achiever's Strategy

We live in tough times, what I've called a "decade of daring." It's a time that belongs to the bold, not the fainthearted. Global confrontation is taking place, and we must have a world perspective. The planet earth has become a neighborhood to those on it. The world needs men with godly wisdom to penetrate the arts, media, business, systems of jurisprudence and government.

One of the reasons we lack leaders with the spirit of a Daniel is found in the parable of the "Bramble Bush," Judges 9, given by Gideon's son.[16] When Gideon died, an evil son tried to slay all the other sons in order to take his father's place. Gideon's lone son who survived the pogrom indicted the new king as being worthless and the worst among them. Using trees as a metaphor, he said the trees called to the olive tree to come rule over them. It refused, not wanting to leave its "fat life." Enjoying its riches, comfort and success, the olive tree did not want to take up the hardship, grueling demands and rigors such leadership required.

The other trees next appealed to the fig tree. It did not want to leave its "sweet life." It preferred to avoid confrontation, escape truth and indulge in pleasure. It wanted its life with "no demands," so it also rejected the call to leadership.

Next, they asked the grapevine, but it had a "full life." Life was one big arcade to be played. Wanting to avoid risk, motivated by a fear of failure, averting reality and knowing that, when fermented, its grapes could cause inconsistency in responsibility, the grapevine also declined the call to leadership.

Finally, the trees called to the bramble bush, which led an "empty life." The bush was vain, rootless and willing to grow and blow anywhere. It had no sense of direction. Its life was one of fruitlessness. It had no sense of shame because of its barrenness. In the nature of moral and immoral, it was amoral, without moral quality. When called to leadership, it eagerly accepted. Once in power, it became haughty, arrogant and demanding of others but not of self.

When the better trees refused leadership, the worst among them accepted. For olive trees, fig trees and grapevines to complain about the quality of leadership would have been foolish. Their rejection of the appeal to lead subordinated them to the inadequate, inferior and insufficient—the literate to the illiterate.

Apply this to our day, when men of ability, quality, character, morality and acuity refuse to seek or accept leadership roles. We then complain when men of lesser stature attain positions of power. By abandoning moral responsibility in the community, men make way for the criminal element to rise. Abandonment of responsibility is the surest way for good men to capitulate to criminal commission. Weakness ascends when strength abdicates.

Leadership at any level can be a lonely life. Martyrdom is never a chosen profession. But it's better to have something worth dying for than to have nothing worth living for. Men must be scripturally literate to be strong in the face of immoral leadership and to rise to moral leadership.

End Thoughts

- Counselors determine the destiny of kings.
- A man without an organized system of thought will always be at the mercy of the man who has one.
- Knowledge of God's Word is a bulwark against deception, temptation, accusation, even persecution.
- Weakness ascends when strength abdicates.
- Wisdom produces a strategy that leads to victory, resulting in glory.

Reflections

1. Whom do you know who comes closer to being a "walking Bible" because they know it so well?
2. Which leaders in your government today uphold biblical principles? Are some leaders unaware of them? Do some purposely defy them?
3. How would knowledge of the Bible keep men from following trends and help them influence their communities? How can it help you?

TEN

THE POWER OF A FOUR-LETTER WORD

"Doctors bury their mistakes; preachers live with theirs," goes an old saying. Some of my gaffes have lived with me through the years, indelibly etched on my mind.

One time, for instance, I was addressing a ladies' group and made the statement, "Sex and prayer are similar in that so many talk about it, but so few do it." The tension my words created made me sense a kindredness to the Hebrews in the fiery furnace. I was thankful the Lord was with me then as He was with them. (I still think that statement makes a valid point about prayer, but I've learned to gear my terminology more to the audience.)

Recently, I heard a man describe "prayer abuse," and I again thought of the analogy to sex. Sexual abuse is generally caused by lust, and so is prayer abuse. "You ask amiss, that you may spend it on your pleasures," James counseled.[1] Prayer, like both money and sex, was made for loving and giving, not for lusting and getting.

Daniel's difficult life was marked by prayer. He knew how and what to pray–a sign of wisdom. In prayer and meditation, he learned God's secrets. "Friendship with God is reserved for those who reverence him. With them alone he shares the secrets of his promises."[2] A man doesn't fall in love in a crowd but alone with the one he loves. Daniel loved God. His highest enjoyment was fellowship with the Father. Knowing when it was trysting time with God was paramount in the time management of his life. "Reverence for God adds hours to each day."[3]

As a student and later as a civic leader, each with specific demands, Daniel had to balance his time. The wonder of prayer, when placed first in life, makes other things go so much easier.

Knowing when to study, pray, work, attend meetings, relax and enjoy recreation is something learned. The secret to life's success is purpose, planning, preparation, production. Not only does failure to plan produce stress personally, but the stress is compounded in others. I've watched men ruin marriages, businesses and ministries by the stress produced through procrastination and indecision. The anxiety and strain resulting from haphazard, arbitrary or aberrant work habits and family concerns makes life too arduous. More often than not, it indicates a high degree of selfishness.

When prayer does not receive first priority, matters seem to be more laborious and much more time-consuming. Meditation is the matrix of creativity. Quiet reflection in light of God's Word rejuvenates the flow of creative ideas, gives new perspectives to issues and insight into people and reduces monstrous problems to miniscule matters that can be controlled.

Time has quality more than quantity. Men who believe they have a large quantity of time fail to value its quality and waste it or try to "kill time." That's time abuse.

A prayer pattern is necessary to designing a meaningful life. The New Testament records five basic prayers.

The Sinner's Prayer

In Christ's parable of the Pharisee and publican who revealed their natures through their prayers, the publican, rather than the Pharisee, was justified. The religious man was eloquent, experienced and polished, but his prayers never got beyond his human audience. The publican was humble, penitent and believing, and his prayers reached the highest Heaven. "Be merciful to me a sinner," he petitioned.4 Pardon was granted.

The Pharisee's prayer constituted a high degree of prayer abuse, centered in self and self-righteousness. The publican's prayer was centered on God and His grace, a true sinner's prayer, marked by godly sorrow that begets repentance and leads to faith.

The Disciple's Prayer

Generally referred to as The Lord's Prayer because He gave it as a model of prayer, it's really the disciples' prayer because He gave it to them when they requested, "Teach us to pray."[5] It's a pattern in prayer that embraces the totality of a man's life and God's will on earth.

The Lord's Prayer

Jesus' supplication in the Garden of Gethsemane was a prayer so intense it caused sweat like great drops of blood on His forehead. It is a prayer of submission, a total investment of His life in the will of God the Father. "Not my will, but thine, be done."[6]

The sinless Son of God was facing the most reprehensible moment of His life, being made sin for us. Tasting our death. Separation from the Father. Tested to the depths of His consecration and faith. His greatest act of faith was not in the miracles He did, but in trusting the Father to raise Him from the dead, not because He doubted the Father, but because He had never tasted death.

His prayer facing the crucifixion is a pattern for us when we are forced to face death-dealing blows like divorce, bankruptcy or criminal prosecution. Submission to the will of God does not guarantee there will be no death, but that after death, there will be a resurrection.

The Intercessor's Prayer

The high-priestly prayer of Jesus was the benediction for His life here on earth and His intercession for you and me.[7] Selflessness, concern for the benefit of the one loved and a desire for unity are the evidences of God's love.[8] These were the characteristics revealed in His intercession. They are the marks of the intercessor. They are also the evidences of a man's love for his family.

Intercession is the best way to be sensitive to others' needs. The Spirit of God knows more about people than we could discover in a lifetime. Motivated by love, filled with compassion, exercising faith, intercessors with the mind of Christ have God's perspective of what will be, not what is. They look at things that are not, rather than things that are. To the intercessor, prayer is the womb in which the Spirit conceives what is later birthed into the world.

The Devil's Prayer

When Jesus entered one of the synagogues, a man with an unclean (demonic) spirit cried out, "Let us alone; what have we to do with thee, thou Jesus of Nazareth?"[9] The spirit of the devil did not want to be tormented by the presence of God.

"Just leave me alone" is the devil's prayer that takes many forms both in word and deed. Daniel's detractors and persecutors were tormented by his righteousness. His convictions, unshakable and immovable, were a rebuke to their preferences, which were weak and negotiable. Their prayer was to be left alone by Daniel, in whom the Spirit of God dwelt. It was manifested in their lust to remove and destroy him.

The Benchmark of Prayer

For years, various groups have ministered to the athletes of America, with marvelous results. Some of the most outstanding players are genuine lovers of God. Unashamed of Jesus, they are bold in publicly identifying with Him. The media, and especially the television networks, used to want these spiritually-strong stars to leave them alone. When men or women from opposing teams kneel to pray at the center of the field or court after a game is over, many television directors still attempt to show as little of this bold and brotherly action as possible.

A change came about, I believe, because of an incident after one particularly humiliating defeat for the Philadelphia Eagles football team. An Eagle at the time, and one of the finest defensive ends ever in American football, Reggie White walked into the locker room, sat down and hung his head. Before he could collect his thoughts, a microphone and camera were thrust in front of him.

"What do you think of the loss?" one news reporter asked him.

"Jesus is still Lord," Reggie replied.

The microphone jerked away, recorders clicked off, the camera lens backed up, and Reggie turned for the first time to see those who were behind the equipment.

"Isn't that just like the devil!" Reggie called after them.

"You mention the Name of Jesus Christ, and he just runs away."

Challenged, the media group came back to finish the interview. Reggie began demanding that if they wanted the interview, they would have to let him talk about Jesus. Reggie has remained as fanatical about Jesus behind the scenes as he ever was in front of the camera, and he is one of my personal friends and heroes.

Strength in prayer gives moral strength to character.

At times, over the years, I have been privileged to observe closely the lives of great men in action. Without question, the ability to pray is the benchmark of their lives. I love to hear men pray who are talking to God and not just performing for the benefit of listening bystanders. They are men who know how to "move the arm of God in prayer."

At times, in public worship services I have attended, the men's prayers have been an embarrassment to Christian masculinity. Their prayer lives seemed afflicted with spiritual anemia.

When this ministry to men first began, I was amazed to discover how inconsistently men pray with their wives. They evidently don't know the scriptural principle that *prayer produces intimacy*. You become intimate with the One *to* whom you pray, *for* whom you pray and *with* whom you pray.

"If two of you shall agree on earth as touching any thing ..." is God's promise.[10] Praying together gives the strength of intimacy to any relationship. That bonding helps to hold the marriage together in tough times.

Private prayer brings boldness in public appearances. Boldness is the missing element in the majority of Christian men. Boldness was the quality of life in the apostles that caused people to say that they were the ones who had "turned the world upside down."[11]

Private prayer brings boldness in public appearances.

Daniel's boldness was exhibited in more ways than one. He was bold in faith, in public identity with Jehovah, in prayer, in friendships and in facing lions. He was bold, not brash. People admire boldness and despise brashness.

"The wicked flee when no man pursues them," the Proverb says, "but the [uncompromisingly] righteous are bold as a lion."[12]

The power of prayer is not limited by space or time. Prayers that reach Heaven can also reach around the world.

One reason why men are not as keen to pray as women is that prayer is based on a personal relationship, and women tend to be better at relationships than men. Men were given stewardship over the earth, so they tend to be fulfilled by impersonal things. Women were created to be the completion of the man and are basically fulfilled in personal matters. Women's books and magazines usually deal with relationships. Men more often read news, business, sports and how-to manuals. Men who become vigorous in prayer are effective because they work at it.

The Word is a rock, faith is a substance, and prayer is a platform. They all uphold you.

Prayer never comes naturally. The natural man is not given to prayer except in crisis. Initially, life is not spiritual but natural, and so it is with prayer.[13] The spiritual man puts the spiritual life first and then the natural. The mark of the spiritually potent person is prayer.

Spiritual Muscle

The practice of lifting people up in prayer produces spiritual muscle. Developing strength in prayer is necessary for the tough times ahead.

Tough is:

- when you are working and taking care of two small children while your wife is dying with cancer.

- when your wife tells you she is pregnant with another man's child.
- being told your newborn infant will never be normal.
- going to prison for your partner's crime.
- recovering from substance and sex abuse.
- having a police officer at the door, saying your lovely daughter has just been paralyzed in an accident caused by a drunk driver.
- knowing the drunk driver will be back at work in six months, but you may never get your daughter back.

Alcohol can never soothe the pain and hurt the way God can. *Drugs are an escape to bondage, while prayer is an escape to freedom.* Being mad at God, maintaining a grudge against Him for some perceived injustice, means cutting yourself off from your only source of help. Prayer is the place where you can ask why and get an answer from the Master. Prayer is the avenue to vent every hurt, anger, sorrow and frustration and have Jesus Christ minister to your needs.

"He Himself [in His humanity] has suffered in being tempted (tested and tried), He is able [immediately] to run to the cry of (assist, relieve) those who are being tempted and tested and tried [and who therefore are being exposed to suffering]."[14]

Run to the heart of God, not from Him. He meant for you to "cast all your care upon" Him or He wouldn't have said it.[15] Trying to be "good" in the presence of God is a prideful and pharisaical effort. *You don't get good and then get to God; you get to God, and He makes you good!*

You may be sound in willpower, muscular strength, moral fiber or mental toughness, but being vibrant in prayer is greater. The absence of prayer is testimony to your ability. The presence of prayer is testimony to God's ability.

The most powerful four-letter word you'll ever learn is P-R-A-Y!

End Thoughts

- Prayer, sex and money were made for loving and giving, not lusting and getting.
- Submission to the will of God does not guarantee that there will be no death but guarantees that after the death, there will be a resurrection.
- Prayer produces intimacy. You become intimate with the One *to* whom you pray, *for* whom you pray and *with* whom you pray.
- Men tend to be fulfilled in things impersonal, women in things personal.
- You don't get good and get to God; you get to God, and He makes you good.
- The absence of prayer is testimony to your ability; the presence of prayer is testimony to God's ability.

Reflections

1. What was the first prayer you ever learned?
2. How often do you believe Jesus prayed? Why did He pray?
3. How is your life structured? Do you make time to be with family? to have recreation? to pray?

ELEVEN

WAKE UP, DAD!

Brandon came with me to Austin, Texas, for a Sunday meeting. Bright-faced, tow-headed and with eyes like sparkling blue gems, my nine-year-old grandson seemed ready to start traveling with me as his father had years earlier. I want to bond with my grandchildren, and the best way is to be alone with them man-to-man (or woman).

Saturday night in our hotel room, I had Brandon read the Bible for our devotional time. When he finished, we knelt side by side next to the bed, and I began to pray my nine-year-old prayer. "Lord, bless Brandon's father and mother," I began. When I finished, I invited Brandon to pray.

From the corner of my eye, I watched as his small frame knelt uprightly in an attitude of worship, hands folded, serene face looking upward with closed eyes, the glow of the lamp reflecting his light spray of freckles. Then he began. "Lord, we know the whole world lies with the wicked one and that Jesus Christ came to save us, so we pray for the men we will minister to tomorrow. Station the angels of Heaven around us and protect us ...." On he went with his spiritual-warfare, sixty-year-old prayer. I still laugh at the incongruity. I thought I'd pray, "Now I lay me down to sleep," and my nine-year-old grandson was in a real prayer mode. It made me appreciate his parents more.

His brother, Bryce, accompanied me to Tulsa two years later and did equally well. Prior to our Christian Men's Event, the pastors and others involved met to pray privately in a room near the stage area. As the august brethren gathered around the table to join me in intercession, Bryce took his place at my side. As with Brandon, we made up the Cole Evangelistic Team that day, and his job was to read the Bible text before I spoke to the crowd. After the others prayed, I asked Bryce to take his turn.

Somberly and seriously, he started in. "Lord, if there are any men here today that don't know how to kiss their sons at night before bed or don't know how to pray with them, please help them do it."

The simple reality in his prayer touched us all. When we left to start the meeting with Bryce walking straight and tall, carrying his Bible, I could not help but thank God for the salvation that was first in my mother, then in me, then in his parents and now is birthed in him. John, the "beloved apostle," wrote, "I have no greater joy than to hear my children walk in truth."[1]

Allen brought his fifteen-year-old son to that men's meeting to spend the day with him. At one point during the day, we asked men who wanted to make things right with God to come to the front. As I saw Allen Jr. standing with his father near the stage, so intensely serious, I asked why he came.

"Because I wanted God to forgive me for being mad at Him for taking away my mother," he answered. She had died just a few years earlier.

His admission was so genuine and meaningful. In a spontaneous gesture to confirm his manhood, we gave him some money to take the family to dinner the next day to tell them what God had done in his life. He chose the restaurant, asked the blessing and told the waiter he'd be responsible for the bill.

During dinner, he told his family what happened the day before and asked his stepmother to forgive him for the way he had acted toward her. He had invited her parents to join them, and now his stepgrandfather stood, came around to him and hugged the young man. By this time, most at the table were crying–his sisters, whose lives had been so tragically affected by the loss of their mother and emotionally affected by their brother's resistance to the new stepmother; his father, who had struggled to bridge the gulf between stepmother and son; his stepgrandparents, who watched in sadness as their daughter struggled to blend two families.

As the family cried, forgave and hugged, diners at other tables listened in and began to cry with them. "I'm so proud of you," said a stranger who came to their table to hug Allen Jr.

An incredible, wonderful work of reconciliation and family unity took place that Sunday at dinner. One young man's forgiveness, brought through the tearful prayers of his parents, affected the lives of others around him immediately and who knows how many more in the years to come.

You're never too young to be taught and never too old to teach. *Hearing from God doesn't depend on age but on relationship.*

Daniel is believed to have been fifteen years old when he was carried away captive to Babylon. In the culture of his childhood home, he had already entered manhood at age thirteen. One aspect of his maturity was revealed in his acceptance and adjustment to the changes in his life. Resilience is a characteristic of strength.

Joseph, son of Jacob, set the precedent, and it's also recorded in the Old Testament. After dreaming of greatness at age seventeen, Joseph was sold down the river by his brothers. What appeared to be evil turned to good,

Hearing from God doesn't depend on age but on relationship.

however, by God's transcendent glory. Starting as a slave in the foreign land of Egypt, Joseph rose to a position of prominence and authority. When his famine-starved family later appealed to Egypt for food, Joseph was there, and because of him, Pharaoh showed Israel favor. What appeared to be such a detrimental incident in Joseph's life actually became part of God's preparation to care for both him and the other Israelites.[2]

Though both men lived through tough times, there is no record that at any time Joseph or Daniel murmured against God for what befell them. God's ways are higher than ours, just "as the heavens are higher than the earth."[3]

Eking out a living for forty years on the back side of the desert served to temper and tame Moses, just as prison and Potiphar's house strengthened Joseph, and the king's house prepared Daniel. The present is merely preparation for the future. But the future never really comes. Just as it finally arrives, it becomes the present. *The past is gone, the future never comes, so we're left with only the present.*

Never Too Soon to Start

Daniel stood before the king at age seventeen and not only interpreted a dream but was willing to declare the whole counsel of God without fear. His education, training and discipline as a child prepared him for the manhood of his teens. His parents must have been diligent in their stewardship of Daniel's life through early adolescence; otherwise, he would not have been ready to stand on his own beliefs and convictions. Since "the godly ... in the land ... are the true nobility,"[4] Daniel came from noble parents.

Men must prepare their children today for the day when they will be called upon to live by their own standards without parental support. We cannot afford to assume our children will grow up in circumstances like our own. They must be trained and their character prepared to sustain them through the toughest of days.

Author Tom Wolfe said, "Blue collar Americans have become morally naked. When the working class threw away the morals their parents gave them, they tried to imitate the worst of the wealthy. Which means you don't have to obey ethical bounds of monogamy or the rules against pornography." He concluded that what he called the new American decadence was begat by the affluence of its society.5

James Lincoln Collier, the author of *The Rise of Selfishness in America,* said, "Selfishness shows up particularly in the abandonment of our children. We feel that we have a right to have kids, and then we put them in day-care centers. We don't even try to give them two resident partners."6 In the US right now, nearly 40 percent of children are born without fathers at home. We spend $4.5 billion a year on pornographic phone calls, and pay baseball players $8 million a year. We spend $150 billion a year for illegal drugs, $114.2 billion per year for health-related care due to drug use and $50 billion to mount a war on drugs. We spend $88.8 billion for tobacco, $97 billion for alcohol and $313 billion per year for treatment of alcohol and tobacco-related medical problems. We spend $586 billion on gambling and only $497 billion for education.

James Dobson, the preeminent Christian apologist for the family, wrote, "It is difficult to overemphasize the negative impact music is having [on our children]. [Here are] the words that appeared in one album:

226 uses of the 'F' word
117 explicit terms for genetalia
87 descriptions of oral sex
163 uses of the word for female dog
17 uses of 'ho' (slang for whore)
81 uses of the 'S' word."[7]

It takes a real man to raise his children today in the nurture and admonition of the Lord.[8] He must have spiritual stamina to fight day by day against the onslaught of the world's corruption. Stepparents must be especially strong to cope with the attitudes of children when they are suffering dislocation, rejection and identity crisis. *As God parents us, so we parent the children He entrusts to our care.*

God did not deny Adam the fruit of that one tree to deprive him of enjoyment but to keep him from destroying himself. God's will was not for Adam's hurt but for his good. Likewise, God has not asked us to resist the world and forgo its pleasures to restrain our happiness but that we might live and not die. There *is* pleasure in sin, but it lasts only for a season.[9] After that are the consequences that can last a lifetime or even an eternity. Godly parents don't discipline their children's appetites for pleasure because they dislike their children but because they love them.

In another book, I wrote about "fabulous fathers and deadly dads." But the new phenomenon with divorce is deadbeat dads. Many times, these men are merely moral mutants, cowards or macho-type procreators without any sense of responsibility. They cause people to assume that all men are inherently unreliable. That's patently unfair, of course. However, the fact remains that irresponsible males who reject the honorable and ethical course of support for their children and let the entire burden rest on the woman are a curse on our world.

Nicholas Davidson, in his book *The Failure of Feminism*, wrote, "Fifteen million American children, one-quarter of the population under 18, are growing up today without fathers. This social catastrophe is at the root of epidemics of crime and drugs, it is deeply implicated in the decline in educational attainment, and it is largely responsible for the persistence of widespread poverty despite generous governmental support for the needy.

"The negative effect of absent fathers on educational attainment occurs regardless of income level. A major study ... [resulted in the researchers concluding] that 'one-parent children on the whole show lower achievement in school than do their two-parent classmates.' This suggests that the decline in American educational performance over the past generation has more to do with the quality of families than with the quality of schools."[10]

Absentee fathers are causing society to pay a high price for their low living.

Men hoping, working, studying and wanting to be good husbands and fathers have their own stress in life–the balance between work and home. Though faced with the pressure to be more involved with their child's upbringing at home, the economy is forcing more men to spend more time providing for the family. Men are working harder to make less money than in years past. The inability to give time is producing guilt and increasing the tension between family members.

"I would feel terrible if my daughter took her first baby steps at the day-care center and not at home," one father recently told me.

He is one of a new type of dad who, according to the Bureau of National Affairs, is more apt to visit the children at school, be involved with picking them up, transporting them places and helping with the homework.[11] Paradoxically while signs, facts and figures tell of the decay of family life, there's a resurgence of concern and a concerted effort to strengthen family life. Fathers have always been willing to put their children's lives above their own in an emergency situation like a fire. But there's a growing desire among Christian men to translate that love into their daily priorities.

The Evidences of Love

The blood covenant of friendship revealed in Scripture meant each covenant partner was willing to give his own life or dearest possession for the other. What belonged to one belonged to the other. For example, fathers in Oriental lands (which includes the land of the Bible) prized their sons' lives more than their own. To die without a son meant life was a failure. If a father had a choice between his own life or his son's, he would rather surrender his own life.

Nowhere is this principle more clearly demonstrated than in God's covenant with Abraham. Abraham's hopes centered in Isaac, his child and heir, the son of promise. It was easier for Abraham to offer up his own life before God than to be asked to give up his son. Yet God required Abraham to offer his son on an altar. At the last moment, however, God provided a substitute sacrifice and freed Isaac. God proved Abraham to be His friend by asking for Isaac. Abraham proved God his friend by giving Isaac. Nothing Abraham did could be greater than showing his faith in God's covenant promise by offering Isaac on the mount as a sacrifice.[12]

"Greater love hath no man than this, that a man lay down his life for his friends," Christ said.[13] Abraham did more—he was willing to lay down his son's life. In so doing, he foreshadowed the love of God, who gave His only begotten Son at Calvary. *God's love is unconditional, sacrificial and redemptive.* Those in covenant relationship with Him through Christ are to manifest those same characteristics. This is how a man is to love his family.

Love for the family begins between husband and wife and includes children when they come into the family. A man is to love his family even as Christ loves the Church. There are both evidences and provisions in that love. The evidences of God's love are selflessness, the desire to benefit the one loved and a desire for unity.

Selflessness: God gave His only Son. Christ pleased not Himself but the Father. The Holy Spirit magnifies Christ, not Himself. Selflessness is the essence of God's nature. "God so loved the world, that he gave …."[14]

Desire to benefit the one loved: God gave Christ that we might have everlasting life. Christ came into the world to seek and save the lost. The Holy Spirit works all things for our good—to develop Christlikeness in us.

Desire for unity: God's purpose in redemption is to adopt us into His family. Christ prayed that we might be one with Father. The Holy Spirit makes us part of the Body of Christ.

The Provisions of Love

The provisions of love are identity, security and stability.

Identity: We are identified with Christ by His Word, His blood and His Spirit. When a man marries a woman and gives her his name in the exchange of matrimonial vows, he gives her his identity. In taking his name, she becomes identified with his character. She must be pleased with his identity or at least feel compatible with it.

Conversely, loss of respect is the underlying cause of most troubled marriages in America.[15] If a woman cannot respect a man, she won't want to bear his name. A man's name is as good as his word.

A man in Colorado stood before a group of men and admitted his wife wanted a divorce. Because of his odious reputation in the community, she was excluded from her old friendships, and their children were teased unmercifully. He asked for forgiveness; she wanted restitution. He wanted instant reunion; she wanted consistent evidence of change. He gave his word; she wanted proof. He constantly denied her charges, but as the Proverb says, "You can't heal a wound by saying it's not there!"[16] His name was not a fragrance to her but a stench.

On the other hand, a woman gets great satisfaction and pride from a husband's name that reflects well upon her. Wearing his name is like a badge of honor, something to be appreciated and held in high esteem. As a tasty dish is savored, so are the kind comments and compliments she hears about her husband. *A man may give his wife a mink coat to wear, but his name is her best covering.*

Why do some women want to remain single? They prefer their own name to one they disdain. Why do some children rebel? From shame in bearing their father's name. It's more than a stain on clothing; it is a blot on their lives. "A child's glory is his father," Proverbs says.[17]

What is your reputation with your wife and children? How do they feel about being identified with your name?

Security: God has made covenant with us in Christ. There's an old adage: "A woman's security is in her home." That's partially true but not completely. When a woman marries, her security is first and foremost in her husband. He is the *Jehovah Jireh* in the home, the provider.

His provisions are not merely the tangibles of food, clothing and shelter but also the intangibles of direction, protection and correction. He provides a legacy for his family in more ways than monetarily by what he has invested in their lives and spirits. Insecurity in his manhood translates into insecurity in his family's life, especially his wife's. That insecurity creates an anxiety that is expressed in nagging, criticism and faultfinding. For her to confront him directly would impugn his manhood, make him defensive and build emotional and communication barriers that might never be surmounted.

As for the tangibles, men with a "renter's mentality" never see the importance of providing by buying a home. Women want something they can call their own, fix up, decorate and give their personal touch. Renting generally cannot provide them with the same sense of security that satisfies their "nesting" instinct.

Security also comes from recognizing and adhering to familial rights of possession and expectation. Let me explain. My son was in the fifth grade when he brought home a report card that was less than satisfactory. When I questioned him as to why he had not done better, he answered with a shrug, "What do you expect?" Well, I told him what I expected in no uncertain terms. You see, a child has a right of possession in having parents. From that he also has the right of expectation. He has the right to expect that his father will provide him with food, clothing and shelter and that his mother will make those daily provisions available. But these rights work both ways. Parents have the right of possession to their children, and they have the right to expect something from them, too.

God has the right of possession to our lives, and from that, we have the right of expectation from our heavenly Father. We pray and expect an answer. We have needs and expect Him to meet them. That is our right as part of the family of God (physically created in His image and spiritually recreated into one of His children). By the same token, God has the right to expect us to believe Him, obey His Word, keep His commandments, do His will and become Christlike.

Stability: Our lives are built on the Rock–Christ Jesus. An oak tree is strong enough to withstand storms because its underground roots spread out as far as the branches do above ground. It is rooted. Stable. Unmovable. Strong.

Changing jobs, jumping from one get-rich-quick scheme to another, sporadically moving to look for work and even church-hopping are not demonstrations of stability. And at the extreme, abusiveness indicates insecurity in manhood and emotional instability. Often illiteracy contributes to instability.

Children raised in an unstable environment are at risk in adulthood. Maurice wrote me, "I only paid lip service to my commitment to God and my wife, who suffered greatly from my lack of compassion toward her and indifference to her needs ... Then I heard a man say, 'If your marriage fails, blame yourself,' and it caused me to be filled with guilt. I began to pray over it and asked God to change my heart. He did. I don't know why I was blind for so long. I can't undo the past, but I intend to let God take care of the future. I'm a blessed man."

Giving lip service to God is hypocritical and causes instability in all of a man's ways. Men thereby hurt themselves and aggrieve their families as well. Renewing our minds with the Holy Spirit, stabilizing our emotions through His love and establishing our hearts in His Word are essential to the stability needed in good fathering.

Marriage is so serious that it's good we can laugh about it occasionally. The man in the airport had his wedding ring on his right hand, so a man sitting nearby said, "You're wearing your wedding ring on the wrong hand."

"Nope," he replied, "married the wrong woman."

Marriage and family can be sources of laughter or tears. Both are under severe attack by a phalanx of destructive forces seeking to eliminate them. Since God created them, however, destroying them would require destroying God Himself.

I read an amusing story about a young man who joined one of London's older gentleman's clubs. On a visit one day, he sat down next to an older, austere gentleman. Wanting to be friendly, he offered, "May I buy you a cigar?"

"Nope. Tried it once, didn't like it, never tried it again," the gentleman answered.

Rebuffed but not daunted, the younger man tried again. "May I buy you a drink?"

"Nope. Tried it once, didn't like it, never tried it again," was the brusque reply.

After a moment, the young man tried again. "How about a game of cribbage?"

"Nope," said the older man again. "Tried it once, didn't like it, never tried it again." After a pause, he continued, "However, my son will be here shortly, and he might like a game."

"Your only child, I presume!" said the younger man.

The Current Crisis

More and more women today are choosing to have children without husbands. Many women now view men simply as sex objects, the very thing they object to in men's regard for them. Often they have the contemptuous attitude that men are needed only for their sperm. When interviewed, their common complaint is that there aren't any stable men who are willing to be committed to a family. Involved, yes. Committed, no.

It's well known that the largest percentage of juvenile delinquents come from fatherless homes. Yet many women are willing to take on the task of being sole bread winner, nurturer, disciplinarian and role model, with all the risks and burdens that entails, because it seems easier than rearing a man while rearing the kids. Immature males make incompatible husbands. In a report on the 1,178,000 marriages that broke up in 1986, women filed more than 61 percent of the petitions for divorce.[18]

A new survey states that more than half our teenage mothers were molested as children. Of those, 94 percent knew the abusers, and 25 percent of the abusers were family members. The abusive experience makes victims feel hopeless and overcome with the attitude that "it just doesn't matter."[19]

A noted activist for the poor found that they were most concerned, not with utility bills or trash collection, but with family life.[20] *Statistically, fatherlessness is more closely associated with crime than either race or poverty.* Intact poor families are unlikely to produce criminals, but well-off broken families may very well do so.[21]

In the Los Angeles race riots of 1992, when the whole world watched the catastrophic conflagration by television, reports said they were terrorist inspired, gang led but crowd completed. "Crowd mentality" is always dangerous. Gangs have proliferated among young men and women, not only in Los Angeles, where they are estimated at three hundred gangs strong, but throughout the world.

Gangs predominantly derive membership from homes with absentee fathers. Like cults, gangs are counterfeit families. The father's responsibility in the home is to provide intimacy, discipline, love and value. Gangs and cults provide all four.

The four basic desires in life are to be, to beget, to belong and to possess. In desiring "to be," identity is the issue. A person's identity crisis must be resolved to live a normal life. Men who have never resolved it are erratic and ever vacillating. They can provide neither identity nor stability. Of even more gravity is the need for identifying with God in Christ. It's the basic issue of Christianity. But gangs also provide identity. Members think their colors are worth dying for.

The desire to beget means to produce. Productivity is the fulfillment of life. When women beget children, they find fulfillment.

Men find it bringing in the harvest. Children discover it in learning. The Church enjoys it when others are born into the family of God. Gangs provide productivity and reproduce themselves, making initiation a coveted rite of passage.

The desire to belong is fulfilled in finding acceptance, becoming attached. An informal survey by a social service to young prostitutes in Hollywood reported that almost 100 percent of them, both male and female, were sexually molested, and almost 90 percent of them were disowned by their families.[22] Unwanted. Being without a family meant they felt worthless. The family of God is the ultimate belonging that gives satisfaction. Gangs provide this also. Belonging to the "brotherhood" is a deep attachment that gives meaning to life.

The desire to possess is satisfied when you can call something your own, whether it's a dog, cat, blanket, car, degree, house, business or whatever. Eternal life is the ultimate possession. Nothing, including fame or fortune, is greater. But here again, gangs provide a substitute in the possession of shoes, coats, hats and especially guns.

Family life gives personal fulfillment to the individual. God created the family for that purpose. Where such fulfillment is absent, counterfeit families, under the aegis of the great counterfeiter, Satan, will provide it. It's no wonder there are so many denominations, clubs, organizations, parties and groups for people to join. People are social creatures and need fulfillment. The home and church are the places God intends for us to find the greatest sense of fulfillment.

It's tough:

- when your son or daughter leaves to live in a cult.
- when your son is arrested for a drive-by shooting, the initiation rite into gang membership.
- when your child dies, and you spend a lifetime regretting you were too busy to spend time with him.
- when you discover Christ after your children are grown and gone.
- being a single mom with four boys.

The only source for strength to parent properly in these tough times is Jesus. He has promised us His Spirit to be our Comforter, the One called alongside.[23] He will be our strength in tough times.

Drugs and alcohol are counterfeit comforters. They pick you up only to let you down. The Holy Spirit will undergird you with His infinite power without let down because He is the "lifter up."[24]

As the morality of a society declines and family life disintegrates, men must discipline themselves and their families to prepare for the days ahead. *When the man is gone from the scene, his children will still be in it, living in a far more difficult and dangerous place than he ever knew.*

End Thoughts

- You're never too young to be taught and never too old to teach.
- Hearing from God doesn't depend on age but on relationship.
- The evidences of love are selflessness, the desire to benefit the one loved and a desire for unity.
- The provisions of love are identity, security and stability.

Reflections

1. Would you characterize the family you were raised in as a "normal" family or a "troubled" family? a "good" family or a "bad" family?
2. Joseph and Daniel were both removed from their families in their teens. What did they rely on for a family influence with the evidences and provisions of love?
3. If you have children, are they prepared for the uncertainties that may lie ahead? How can you better prepare them?

TWELVE

A DECADE OF DARING

When my son, Paul, checked into a London hotel, he was shocked to receive a handbill inviting him to a séance in the hotel, along with other handbills inviting him to theaters and restaurants. In much of the world, contemporary society has embraced the occult in the normal flow of life.

Public offerings of psychic phenomena presented on television, tarot and occult displays in malls, spiritism and channeling attracting large crowds and celebrity followings and other such things appear regularly all over the world. Jeanne-Dixon-type seers garner headlines with their predictions of future events. Astrological charts are published in daily newspapers alongside the crossword puzzle, their purveyors making inroads into Buckingham Palace and the White House.

People are fascinated with the future—but only God knows what it holds.

God's prophets recorded their prophecies through the quickening power of His Spirit. False prophets prophesy from their own minds—or from an ungodly source. Prophecies entered into sacred writ in Scripture have been studied, examined and found to be true in exact detail. The prophecies concerning Christ in the Old Testament, true to the "nth" degree in the New Testament, highlight the nature of a true prophet's ministry.

Almost half the book written by Daniel are his prophecies. Theologians, in their study of eschatology (prophecy or "last days"), rely on Daniel's predictions and Apostle John's in the book of Revelation as their major sources.

Prophets both preach and predict. Their preaching is with a "sense of the present," speaking on behalf of God to the people, whereas priests minister from the people to God. Prophets also predict. Daniel had a predictive prophetic vision from God, a revelation of events upon the world, including the foretelling of the second advent of the Messiah.

Historians, theologians and teachers who have studied the book of Daniel agree God accomplished several areas of prime importance through him.[1] First and foremost, he was God's representative in a foreign land to give honor to Jehovah God where it was not normally given. *Honors accorded Daniel were a credit to his God.* Just as important, he prepared a place for the nation of Israel to receive God's blessings. By being in Babylon in a place of power, he was able to secure a favorable status for his people. Additionally, he recorded the revelation that, to this day, is carefully studied for truths about the world's future, which is in God's hands.

Daniel was taken captive in his teens and recorded his final vision over sixty years later. His life proves beyond doubt you're never too young and never too old to be used by the Lord.

The prophetic role is still viable in the Church. A prophetic word in 1979 became such a powerful force in our ministry to men. It was simple but direct. "Sexual sins will be the problem of the church in the 1980s." A prophetic word from 1980 was that our ministry would be "a new sharp threshing instrument having teeth."[2] People thought our emphasis on men odd until the men's movement started ten years later.

What's Happening Now

Scripture's prophesies about the last days are vitally relevant to our day. The Bible predicts there will be:

- compression of time
- acceleration of activity
- magnification of personality
- increase in intensity of living
- deterioration of character
- emasculation of manhood
- erasure of standards
- perversion of principles
- hardening of hearts
- rise of the worship of evil

Sound familiar?

Among other signs of the times, three characteristics of the spirit of the world in the last days must be seriously considered. The Book of the Revelation describes them as:

- lawlessness (from the word "pharmakeia" or drugs)
- impenitence (refusal to confess wrong)
- masochism (inured to violence)

With the worldwide increase in rebellion against constituted authority, with lawlessness in all its variant offenses running rampant, we are witnessing a feature of the last days. Likewise, refusal to admit wrong, lies, guilt, "stonewalling" to prevent truth and the hardness of heart characterized by the rejection of repentance are signs to us. The more we see this and the harder the hearts, the more we realize we are living in what the Bible calls "perilous times."3

Further, when a world society is no longer thrilled by simple sexual escapades but needs "snuff" movies of murderous sex acts; when sado-masochistic practices are advertised as "vogue"; when dance parties maim and cripple; when torture is tolerated; when child pornography fuels the lusts of men to the extent they steal children from their beds to sexually assault then kill them, we can see the beginning of the traits which will proliferate just prior to the second coming of Christ.

Think of the fact that such signs as these are occurring in our times.

Babylon's heyday of advanced culture and world domination during Daniel's period degenerated into catastrophic collapse. One characteristic that presaged its downfall was that "they became as women."4 The feminization of manhood prevailed. Effeminate gestures weren't the problem but rather the abandonment of the manly stewardship of earth. Men forfeited moral leadership and responsibility, became indecisive and left a vacuum that required women to rise to places of power. Our day shows the same symptoms, with the last general election in the United States called "The Year of the Woman."

American leaders testify to a born-again theology but hold to a "liberal" philosophy. The nation is on the verge of a massive change of philosophy based on a change in morality. Change is always certain but not always good.

What the world cannot control, it will decriminalize and legalize. What the church cannot control, it will rationalize and psychologize. What men cannot control, they will demoralize and compromise.

When Daniel wrote his vision, he could not have imagined what our lives would be like in this day. Most who study, interpret and teach prophetically concerning the second advent of Christ somehow emphasize the negative rather than the positive. Volumes have been written about the antichrist, the mark of the beast, tribulation and the end of our world. Too often, the teaching stops there. I believe Daniel also saw the negative but only in light of what he knew of God. *The Lord always builds on a positive.* God always starts on a positive, and He will always end on a positive.

The peace movement received great encouragement, if not its beginnings, from a late, great nuclear scientist. Around the beginning of World War II, he discovered the awesome possibility that a nuclear explosion in the atmosphere might start a chain reaction that could set the heavens on fire and incinerate the earth. The scripturally literate understand the probability of his deduced "possibility" because the Bible speaks of it.

Apostle Peter wrote, "First, I want to remind you that in the last days there will come scoffers who will do every wrong thing they can think of, and laugh at the truth. This will be their line of argument: 'So Jesus promised to come back, did he? Then where is he? He'll never come! Why, as far back as anyone can remember everything has remained exactly as it was since the days of creation.'

> *God always starts on a positive, and He will always end on a positive.*

"They deliberately forget this fact: that God did destroy the world with a mighty flood, long after he had made the heavens by the word of his command, and had used the waters to form the earth and surround it. And God has commanded that the earth and the heavens be stored away for a great bonfire at the judgment day, when all ungodly men will perish."[5]

When the insanity reaches its apex and starts the war-of-all-wars, called Armageddon, with nuclear power unleashed by hatred, prejudice and greed, it could cause the atmosphere to catch on fire. Precious minerals melted therein will run on the face of the earth like streets of gold. The seas will dry up, and the sand will turn to glass. The effect could be the biblical streets of gold and seas of glass. If so, the earth will be purified from sin and become habitable for the redeemed of all ages.[6]

God will end the history of man on earth, not with a negative, but with a spectacular positive.

Prophets, pastors, evangelists and teachers have long controlled and proscribed behavior by propagating the fear that Christ will not come for those attending the theater, football games or recreational activities. But His second coming is not to be a source of dire dread to believers but of great joy, peace and comfort.

Christ is Truth. His Spirit is the Spirit of Truth. When Truth calls, those on earth in whom the Spirit of Truth dwells will rise to be with Him. Let's take the fear out of the place meant for joyous faith!

Judgment Day Is Coming

It's true there will be a day of reckoning, of judgment. It's going to be a tough day for the world and all in it.

If the ungodly commit evil acts while there's still some vestige of morality, decency and godliness in the world, think what is going to happen as that influence decreases.7 The rise of the worship of evil is a conditioning process preparing for what is to come.

"But after thy hardness and impenitent heart treasurest up unto thyself wrath against the day of wrath and revelation of the righteous judgment of God; Who will render to every man according to his deeds:

"To them who by patient continuance in well doing seek for glory and honour and immortality, eternal life:

"But unto them that are contentious, and do not obey the truth, but obey unrighteousness, indignation and wrath, tribulation and anguish, upon every soul of man that doeth evil, of the Jew first, and also of the Gentile."8

Indignation is the proper response to wrong doing. God has a right to be indignant with us when we rebel against doing right in order to do wrong. Wrath is an expression of anger with the deepest of emotion. When the Bible talks about God's indignation and wrath, it makes it clear that those emotions are aimed against men's unrighteousness. The famed lawlessness and judgment of Sodom and Gommorrah were as a pebble to a mountain in comparison with what is to come.

God gives seven principles for the judgment of this world:

1. Judgment will be according to truth.
"But we are sure that the judgment of God is according to truth against them which commit such things."9

2. **Judgment will be according to the accumulated guilt of the individual.**
"But after thy hardness and impenitent heart treasurest up unto thyself wrath against the day of wrath and revelation of the righteous judgment of God."[10]

3. **Judgment will be according to deeds, not intentions.**
"Who will render to every man according to his deeds."[11]

4. **Judgment will be without respect of persons.**
"For there is no respect of persons with God."[12]
Prince or pauper, rich or poor, leader or follower, of any race, nation or generation—God is not partial.

5. **Judgment will be according to performance, not mere knowledge.**
"For not the hearers of the law are just before God but the doers of the law shall be justified."[13]

6. **Judgment will be given according to the Gospel of Christ, not according to psychological precepts or philosophical proclamations.**
"In the day when God shall judge the secrets of men by Jesus Christ according to my gospel."[14]

7. **Judgment will be according to reality.**
"But he is a Jew [or a believer], which is one inwardly; and circumcision is that of the heart, in the spirit, and not in the letter; whose praise is not of men, but of God."[15]

Those are the judgments we can measure ourselves against as we examine our lives in the light of God's Word which pierces "even to the dividing asunder of soul and spirit, and of the joints and marrow, and is a discerner of the thoughts and intents of the heart."[16] These judgments of God were written by Apostle Paul in the New Testament. But centuries earlier, in Hosea's prophesies, God described six reasons for the downfall of Israel.[17]

First, they became the victims of the Canaanite culture around them and compromised their own. Second, they were seduced by pagan worship which seemed more exotic than theirs. Third, Israel believed the Canaanites had the better life. Fourth, they lost the sense of God's presence and purpose. Fifth, they embraced a fertility cult. Sixth, their moral degeneracy led to sanctioned murder. *God considers sanctioned murder to be the worst kind.*

God's judgment is sure for such depravity. In his book, *Cry of the Innocents*, writing of the immorality of sanctioned murder by abortion, the Rev. John O. Anderson explains the types of murder. There is common murder, where somebody does something spontaneously, not out of wrath, hatred or other passion. Then there is the murder of the helpless, done toward those who cannot help themselves. This was the case with Idi Amin of Uganda killing 650,000 people, the Khmer Rouge in Cambodia taking the lives of 2,000,000 and the senseless bloodshed still going on in parts the world.

Then there is murder by official sanction. The Holocaust in Germany during World War II was sanctioned murder. Abortion is the West's holocaust. Sanctioned murder tears a hole in the fabric of a nation that ushers in a spirit of murder which next leads to infanticide, euthanasia, assisted suicide, gang or tribal warfare and even ritual sacrifices, often of babies birthed solely for that purpose. The United States Supreme Court decision on abortion tore a hole in the fabric of American society, and a spirit of murder has overwhelmed this country.

Through the stench of death, however, comes the sweet aroma of life. *The Gospel, with its power to change the vilest person into a saint of God, extends His grace and mercy to the worst among us.* A man in jail sent me a tooled leather Bible cover as a gift of thanks for the messages he's received from book and videotape through the bars of his maximum-security cell. His body is imprisoned but not his spirit, and "where the Spirit of the Lord is, there is liberty."[18]

Who Christians Really Are

Jesus Christ stood before the judgment seat of Pilate who asked Him if He was a king. "Thine own nation and the chief priests have delivered thee unto me," Pilate continued. "What hast thou done?"[19]

Jesus answered him, "My kingdom is not of this world: if my kingdom were of this world, then would my servants fight, that I should not be delivered to the Jews: but now is my kingdom not from hence."[20]

The people who were talking to Pilate made a mistake. They thought of the Messiah as a King who would overthrow the rule of the Roman government, as a deliverer who would lead them from the yoke of the secular government to one of their own religious form. Jesus did not come to change or fight against the secular government, however, but to change the hearts of men, translate them into the Kingdom of God and produce in them His image, Christlikeness.

Christians are called-out ones.[21] Our specific calling on earth is not to focus on secular governments, although, like Daniel, we can influence them. *Our purpose is to reach people with the Gospel of Jesus Christ.* To expend all our energies to try to change governments or establish a new world order is to frustrate the grace of God in our lives.

The Kingdom of God is not of this world. It is not a secular, temporal kingdom but a divine, eternal Kingdom established on earth only in the hearts of men.

A dogmatic secularist said, "Well, you're only preaching a spiritual message. You don't have a social conscience."

To that I say, "Garbage in, garbage out!" The social conscience of this world has always emanated from the Church of Jesus Christ. Philanthropy and benevolence have always started there. What are the most prominent organizations in the world that are devoting money, time, effort, food, clothing and shelter to care for the poor and homeless? They are *Christian* organizations—sustained by the private gifts of people. Love gives. God is love. Love serves. *The people who love God love to serve.*

The Church is not incestuous, either, as some organizations are, willing to serve only its own people. True Christian philanthropy is impartial. *Nothing on earth outgives the Church in its service to humanity.*

What Christians Really Do

The greatest act of philanthropy is the willingness to share the Gospel of Jesus Christ. During my lifetime, I have met some of the finest men God ever put on this earth. They are men I admire, respect and even hold in awe for the way they give the Gospel to their generation.

Men from all over the world attend our Leadership Training Institutes, and each has a story of God's work in his life. None thrilled us more than when Pastor Suliasi Kurulo of Fiji came to a ministry weekend and related his exciting story. Under his leadership, laymen set out to minister systematically to every family in their island nation. For years, they traversed the country on foot and in buses, reaching every individual home with a personal visit and leaving Gospel literature. After completing an entire sweep of the nation twice, they decided to reach the entire South Pacific region surrounding them.

The Fiji laymen—mostly single young men, not pastors or professional ministers—went to the Solomon Islands and met with the brethren there. They set out together to reach each neighborhood, house by house, door by door. Following a strategic map of the islands, they finally came to the border of the murderous Kwaio people in the interior of the island of Malaita.

"This is our next assignment," said the Fijians.

"No, you can't go in there," said the Solomon Islanders.

"We must go in."

"You don't understand," the Solomon Island brothers protested. "Our forefathers have been murdered by these people. The government fears them and has left them alone since 1947. Countless missionaries have gone in, and not one has lived more than three days in Kwaio territory. The church has now turned its back on them. They are so fierce they can't even live near each other, for if they do, they fight to the death. We can't go in."

"We have been sent from Fiji with a special commission to reach every home in the nation of Solomon," the Fijians insisted, "and that includes the Kwaio people. If this journey means we won't return to our own people, we are willing to lay down our lives. We are commissioned by God, not man, and if this is His will, so be it. If we die, we die."

The faith of the Fijians challenged the men of the Solomon Islands. Speaking on behalf of the entire group of laymen, the leader stood and spoke carefully.

"These men have come to care for our people," he said. "How can they care for our people more than we care for ourselves?" Turning to the Fijians, he said, "If you die, we will die alongside you."

For a week, the brethren fasted and prayed together. They prayed for God to give His favor and for the enemy to be silenced and stopped. Then they entered Kwaio territory, climbed the mountains to reach the first village and were taken immediately to knife-wielding tribal leaders. Their lives were in danger at every moment, but the leaders eventually agreed to give them an audience with the high chief, who listened carefully to them. When they were finished, he miraculously did not call for their deaths but believed on Jesus Christ for salvation. After a series of miracles, he then called several villages together to hear the Gospel message, and the revival started.

These young, yet strong men of faith went to the Kwaio in 1989, and today, there are dozens of church buildings standing in the interior of Kwaio territory and thousands of Kwaio believers. These brave and bold men have accepted Christ's commission as the greatest vocation they could know, regardless of their avocation.

Your trade or profession is your *avocation*. Your *vocation* is the call of God to evangelize the world. That is God's primary, fundamental call on your life. *The call to the ministry of Christ, in whatever form, is still the highest and most noble calling on the face of this earth.*

God's anointed pastor is more important than the mayor, governor, president or king. The prime minister, foreign minister, minister of commerce or any other ministry is dwarfed in importance. The ministry of Jesus Christ must not be slandered, as many do, but must be regarded with the highest esteem and respect.

The world today needs men who will acknowledge the call to take the Gospel "into all the world."[22]

The call to the ministry of Christ, in whatever form, is still the highest and most noble calling on the face of this earth.

You have probably never heard the name Wayne Nicholes, but those of us who have met him can never forget him. His life of devotion to His Lord by serving Wycliffe Bible Translators is exemplary. He is one of the finest in God's Army of unsung heroes. For over forty years, he and his wife faithfully taught the Gospel, trained missionaries, administered aid sacrificially and gave themselves unstintingly to others. When I met him in 1980, we became friends.

He promised to support the Christian Men's Network and never missed one month–that is, except for September 1992. That was the month his wife died. He contacted me to tell me of his loss.

"When tender memories of her come up," he wrote, "tears come to my eyes. But they are tears of joy as I reflect on our forty-six years of marriage and as I visualize her there with her heavenly Father, to whom she had always belonged since the day she committed her life to Him and to whom I gave her back at the moment of her death. I believe a real man will weep, not uncontrollably nor mournfully, but as an expression of tender love that only God can give us."

At seventy years of age, his ministry now is to find and recruit younger men, who will have the same desire and passion for Christ. As we talked later, Wayne asked a question that I have often asked others. *Where are the men today who are willing to say, "Jesus, I will leave all and follow You. I will lay down my life for the preaching of the Gospel, to minister to the sick and helpless, the needy, lost and blind. I give my life to You, Jesus"?*

Where is the call to the ministry today in conferences and Gospel meetings? The call to ministry used to result in tens and even hundreds of people standing up in meetings to devote and dedicate themselves publicly to the ministry of Jesus. We considered it a great honor and glorifying to God to give our all. I have been in widely publicized conferences that boasted lists of speakers who are true men and women of God, where thousands of dollars are used to assemble huge crowds of marvelously saved Christians and sinners who meet their Savior–yet there is no call to the ministry. Where is the call to ministry? What have we done with the nobility of serving our God, the Lord and King?

This world is in transition, crisis and confusion. People today need a voice. They need a role model. *The world needs a man who will live an uncompromising life in the midst of a compromising world.*

In these last days, those who know their God will do "exploits" beyond any that have happened in history. What higher calling can a man receive? What greater heritage can a mature Christian man leave? You're never too old or young. What more noble profession could be chosen than to minister the Gospel of Jesus Christ?

This world needs godly men of daring. The old Sunday School tune, "Dare to Be a Daniel," needs to be updated for this new kind of man who truly *dares*. Whatever avocation he may have, he will dare to follow the vocation of serving the Lord.

And will it be tough? Look at Daniel and his friends.

It's tough:

- when you're thrown to lions or into a fiery furnace.
- when people mock your experience with God.
- to start out in ministry and watch your family eat beans for every meal.
- when your dearest friends advise you stop chasing the fantasy of becoming a minister.
- when half your congregation leaves because your message is "too straight."
- to tell your son that if he goes through with a divorce and remarries a woman in the church, they can no longer attend.
- to hear your young daughter say she is pregnant by the deacon's son.
- to be forced out of your church by government action and have no one stand with you.

To answer God's call, to accept the honor-able ministry of Christ, to face adversity, you have to be strong. The people who "know their God" will do exploits. For the men who are rooted and grounded in God's Word, the tough days ahead will be the greatest opportunity of all time to show forth His Glory.

The love of the Truth is the criterion of true Christianity.

The darker the night, the brighter the light.

To start, *you begin where you are with what you have.* Despise not the day of small beginnings.[23]

One of the signs of the last days is that those who refuse Truth in Jesus Christ will be given "strong delusion, that they should believe a lie."[24] Men who love unrighteousness refuse the Truth in Christ and believe falsehoods, whether unchurched or church-going. They will miss Christ's coming because they will be follow-ing after "lying wonders," immoral philosophies, "deeper truths," strange demonstrations and charismatic personalities.[25] It's a tragedy. *The love of the Truth is the criterion of true Christianity.*

An illusion seems real but lacks substance or reality, like a mirage in the desert which men dying of thirst try to reach. It is ever present but never found nor attained. It seems real only because men are deceived. The "image" men will worship in the last days does not have to be physical. It might be more like an illusion.

Only truth is reality. It takes strength to withstand the subtle seductions that would deceive us and lead us to distraction and destruction. They are so sly, so tempting, so appealing–so disastrous. Make sure the signs you follow point to Jesus.

End Thoughts

- Change is always certain but not always good.
- What the world cannot control, it will decriminalize and legalize; what the church cannot control, it will rationalize and psychologize; what men cannot control, they will compromise and demoralize.
- The Lord always builds on a positive; He always starts on a positive and ends on a positive.
- The darker the night, the brighter the light.
- Start where you are with what you have.
- The love of the Truth is the criterion of true Christianity.

Reflections

1. Were you ever interested in movies, books or speakers that claimed to know when or how the earth would end?
2. How did the envy of the Canaanites turn the Israelites off course from following God? What forces today are trying to get you off course?
3. The great evangelist, John Wesley, was asked, "What would you do if you knew Jesus were coming tomorrow?" He answered, "I'd saddle my horse and go to my next meeting." What would you answer?

THIRTEEN

FELLOWSHIP OF THE UNASHAMED

On an Australian ministry tour several years ago, a former football player from the University of Southern California, Tom Sirotnak, was addressing the crowd in our "men-only" event. Quoting from a passage in the Old Testament that forbade men without testicles to enter the Tabernacle, he used the male colloquialism for testicles common to his background to interpret the text as a call for manly courage. "You gotta have [testicles] to be a man!" he shouted bluntly.

I hadn't heard Tom say it quite that way before, so while the men were still in shock, I quickly stood and told them, "We don't say that in our meetings; we say 'spiritual gonads.' "

The men roared in laughter. Although our language was crude, they understood the meaning perfectly.

Say it as politely or as crudely as you want—it is going to take the stuff of real manhood to stand for right, law, order and, above all, godliness in the day and hour we are facing. There are as many men threatened by using the colloquialism for testicles as there are men intimidated by the word godliness. From the beginning, I said this book wasn't for the lazy or for hypocrites. It's for men.

I'm not an angry man. I'm not mad at the world, my father or the government. I'm not angry with people. But I am angry with attitudes, and I'm angry with mediocrity. I'm angry with myself for my sins, and I repent publicly right now, as I have privately before. I'm angry at the cowardice of men who don't have enough backbone to take a stand for Jesus Christ today. I'm angry at the spirit of proud men who rise up in insurrection or stoop down in sedition to topple men of God from the pulpit. I'm angry at the jealousy of ministers who can't stand to see others succeed.

I'm angry at the way men "tsk-tsk" the fresh method that does not fit their mold yet fear to deny the works of God in its results. I'm angry at the complacency that lulls men into accepting less than what Christ paid for at Calvary. I'm angry at the deceit that makes men think remorse or regret are the same as repentance. I'm angry at soft-spirited men who let abortionists take millions in subsidies from the federal government to teach their children "safe sex," how to use condoms and how to get abortions without their parents' consent, yet won't even vote or attend a school board meeting to stand for righteousness.

I'm angry at the arrogance of media who pay scoffers millions of dollars to denigrate Jesus Christ, promote promiscuity, encourage lawlessness and, at the same time, condemn Christian ministries for the monies they raise to get men off drugs, restore marriages and rescue lives from the very perversities they condone.

I'm angry at covetousness in the hearts of men that motivates them to give only to ministries that "bless" them and not to those who are on the front lines for Jesus.

Yes, I am angry. But the apathetic are not.

They have no emotion concerning the issues of our day; no passion for the Gospel; no heart-felt desire to reach the world while there is still time; no willingness to spend their time, talent and treasury for preaching the cross; no desire to lose their lives for Jesus. No, those men are not angry. They are also less than real men, for they have missed the point of God producing the fruit of manhood in their lives.

There is a time for righteous anger. Jesus felt and exhibited it when He found moneylenders in His Father's temple.[1] By doing so, He modeled the righteous anger that is acceptable in God's sight.

There are "moneylenders" today who are ripping off the Church—not only financially, as some would assume, but by lulling us to slumber while the nations are dying; by nullifying our zeal through overtraining to perfection; by dulling our sense of righteousness with programs and plans to make bad people "good" and good people "better"—with no regard for the cross of Jesus Christ and the resurrection power of His blood that transforms those who believe on His Name.

There are board members who have no respect for the Lord's anointed minister; bitter church members who stir up dissensions with no discernment of that which is holy; ignorant preachers who call the Bible "wrong" and fundamentalist believers "bigots"; hateful, so-called believers who kill prophets with their words, thinking they are doing God a service; born-again people who let double-mindedness draw them to charlatans with loose theologies because their approach to Christianity tickles their ears and releases them from walking the straight and narrow road of godliness to salvation.

Coming against these forces, both in the spirit and human realms, requires the spirit of a Daniel. This is not a day for weak-willed, soft-spirited, fleshly-flaccid, half-hearted men who profess the worthy Name of Christ yet don't submit to His Lordship. Compromisers will lose their lives in these perilous times in more ways than one—you can die spiritually, financially, maritally, socially, and a thousand other deaths before you ever die physically.

God's call is to true manhood, which is Christlikeness. His call to men is not to count their lives dear but to count Jesus as more worthy than life itself.

The following pledge comes from uncertain authorship, but I encourage you to make it your own—not by putting a name of authorship at the bottom, but by placing your name at the top and making this inspirational challenge the anthem of every day of your life.

I am a part of the "Fellowship of the Unashamed." The die has been cast. The decision has been made. I have stepped over the line. I won't look back, let up, slow down, back away or be still.

My past is redeemed, my present makes sense, and my future is secure. I'm finished and done with low living, sight walking, small planning, smooth knees, colorless dreams, tamed visions, mundane talking, cheap giving and dwarfed goals.

I no longer need preeminence, prosperity, position, promotions, plaudits or popularity. I don't have to be right, first, tops, recognized, praised, regarded or rewarded. I now live by faith, lean on His presence, walk with patience, live by prayer and labor with power.

My face is set, my gait is fast, my goal is Heaven, my road is narrow, my way is rough, my companions are few, my Guide is reliable, and my mission is clear. I cannot be bought, compromised, detoured, lured away, turned back, deluded or delayed. I will not flinch in the face of sacrifice, hesitate in the presence of the adversary, negotiate at the table of the enemy, ponder at the pool of popularity or meander in the maze of mediocrity.

I won't give up, shut up, let up or slow up until I have stayed up, stored up, prayed up, paid up and spoken up for the cause of Christ. I am a disciple of Jesus. I must go till He comes, give till I drop, preach till all know and work till He stops me. And when He comes for His own, He will have no problem recognizing me. My banner is clear: I am a part of the "Fellowship of the Unashamed."

Be God's man. A member of the "Fellowship of the Unashamed." Raised to new life by Jesus Christ. Having the spirit of a Daniel. A daring man who knows His God and does exploits to glorify His Name.

This is your day!

Reflections

1. Have you ever been angry about something you've seen in the world? Did you try to do anything about it?
2. What new habits must you develop in order to be a strong man?
3. Write out your own creed of what you believe about God and yourself.

NOTES

Chapter 1

1. Proverbs 29:27 TLB
2. 2 Corinthians 3:3
3. Isaiah 51:6
4. Esther 4:14
5. Luke 10:27
6. Job 12:11 TLB

Chapter 2

1. Daniel 1:8
2. Psalm 86:11
3. Psalm 112:8
4. Psalm 53:1
5. Proverbs 23:7
6. Matthew 11:29-30
7. Romans 8:38-39
8. 1 John 5:10 AMP
9. Isaiah 5:14

Chapter 3

1. Proverbs 18:24
2. Acts 11:22, 24
3. 2 Timothy 4:11 AMP
4. Hebrews 11:1
5. Ecclesiastes 11:4 TLB

Chapter 4

1. "Rejecting Religion Hurts Democracy, Theologian Says," *Los Angeles Times*, 10 September 1992, Associated Press news story.
2. From a speech given at a seminar titled "America's Youth: A Crisis in Culture" in Hillsdale, MI, March 1991. Quoted in an article in *Imprimis*, a publication of Hillsdale College, September 1991.
3. *Ibid.*
4. James 1:8
5. Romans 1:32 AMP; Romans 1:30 TLB
6. Reported in a column by Ray Kerrison, *New York Post*, 9 January 1991, p. 2. The journalist was an eyewitness to the incident.
7. *Ibid.*
8. Civil Action No. 92-1824-CIV-T23A, U.S. District Court for the Middle District of Florida, Tampa Division (Orlando, FL: Liberty Council, November 1992).
9. Church invasion source: *National Religion Report* (Roanoke, VA: Media Management, November 1993), p. 5.

Abortion clinic source: *Operation Rescue et al v Women's Health Center Inc. et al*, 626 So. 2nd 664 (FL, 1993), *Orlando Sentinel*, October 29, 1993.
10. *Religious Rights Watch*, Virginia Beach, VA, December 1991.
11. *Ibid.*, July 1990.
12. Matthew 17:21
13. Proverbs 16:32
14. Daniel 5:12
15. Daniel 5:14
16. Galatians 5:19
17. Galatians 4:9
18. 2 Corinthians 5:17; 1 Corinthians 2:16; Romans 8:14
19. Matthew 17:21
20. Galatians 5:25
21. Lee Bueno, *Fast Your Way to Health* (Springdale, PA: Whitaker House, 1991).
22. Hebrews 9:14
23. Hebrews 10:22
24. Acts 24:16

Chapter 5

1. Nancy Wride, "Male-bashing Jokes," *Los Angeles Times*, reprinted in *Dallas Morning News*, 18 October 1992.
2. Philippians 2:13
3. Proverbs 3:32
4. Psalm 37:23; Proverbs 16:9
5. 2 Peter 1:5-7
6. Galatians 6:14
7. Quoted by John Maxwell of Injoy Ministries, Lemon Grove, CA, in the tape series "Stewardship Is Lord," tape 1.
8. Psalm 1:2-3
9. Romans 6:2
10. Galatians 5:19; James 1:14
11. James 4:7
12. Romans 6:11; James 4:7; Romans 8:13; Galatians 1:4
13. Romans 8:13; Colossians 3:5; Romans 6:11
14. Galatians 5:19-21
15. 1 Corinthians 15:31
16. Hebrews 12:1
17. 1 Timothy 6:20
18. Leviticus 19:18-19
19. Revelation 3:16
20. Romans 8:1
21. James 4:10
22. John 16:21
23. Philippians 3:8
24. Luke 6:38
25. Daniel 11:32

Chapter 6

1. Romans 8:29
2. Hebrews 6:13
3. Hebrews 1:3
4. John 14:9 TLB
5. John 1:1
6. John 1:1, 4, 14; 6:51
7. John 1:14
8. Revelation 1:8
9. Romans 10:17
10. Mark 16:17
11. Acts 4:12
12. Matthew 4:4
13. Isaiah 59:12
14. Isaiah 59:13
15. Isaiah 59:14
16. Isaiah 59:14-15
17. "Letters," *Time*, 26 October 1992, p. 6.
18. Genesis 1:26-27
19. Proverbs 18:21
20. Matthew 12:36
21. Job 27:5
22. Job 2:3
23. Psalm 15:4
24. John 8:44
25. John 10:10
26. Numbers 12:3
27. Exodus 8:20
28. 1 Timothy 5:22
29. Mark 4:13-20
30. Acts 17:30
31. Ephesians 4:25

Chapter 7

1. John 15:26
2. 1 Timothy 1:15; Romans 5:8; Romans 4:25.
3. Matthew 18:35
4. Psalm 79:8; Isaiah 43:25
5. James 5:9

Chapter 8

1. *Congressional Record*, 27 July 1987, p. 3081.
2. James 4:17 TLB
3. Matthew 22:37-40
4. James 4:4
5. Ephesians 5:3
6. The acronym is NAMBLA, which stands for North American Man-Boy Love Association.
7. Mike Royko, "Different Treatment of Coach and Sportswriter," *Los Angeles Times*, 20 November 1992.
8. Mark 7:6; Amos 5:21 TLB
9. Matthew 6:22 AMP
10. Numbers 22-24, 31
11. 1 Timothy 4:2
12. Luke 24:49
13. Acts 1:8
14. Psalm 16:3 TLB
15. Psalm 101:6 TLB

Chapter 9

1. Matthew 7:24-27
2. 1 Kings 14; 2 Samuel 16:23
3. John 14:21-23
4. Luke 10:27
5. Cal Thomas, "Beware When Democrats Get Religion," *The Orlando Sentinel*, 27 July 1992.
6. Proverbs 2:4
7. Matthew 25:43
8. Matthew 7:21
9. Daniel 11:32
10. 2 Kings 5; Hebrews 11:6
11. Acts 10:34
12. Mark 3:24-26
13. Ecclesiastes 4:9, 12
14. Proverbs 4:7; 1:7; Proverbs 3:16-17; Proverbs 8:13 TLB; Proverbs 9:10
15. Colossians 2:3
16. "The Parable of the Bramble Bush" I learned from Larry Titus, whose out line I used with his permission. Thank you, Larry.

Chapter 10

1. James 4:3 NKJV
2. Psalm 25:14 TLB
3. Proverbs 10:27 TLB
4. Luke 18:13
5. Luke 11:1
6. Luke 22:42
7. John 17:1-26
8. John 3:16
9. Mark 1:24
10. Matthew 18:19
11. Acts 17:6, 4:13
12. Proverbs 28:1 AMP
13. 1 Corinthians 15:46
14. Hebrews 2:18 AMP
15. 1 Peter 5:7

Chapter 11
1. 3 John 4
2. Genesis 37
3. Isaiah 55:9
4. Psalm 16:3 TLB
5. *Dallas Morning News*, 14 September 1990, Associated Press news story.
6. James Lincoln Collier, *The Rise of Selfishness in America* as quoted in *The Bottom Line*, 30 April 1992. Other statistics were updated in the 2009 printing of this book.
7. "Dr. Dobson Answers Your Questions," *Focus on the Family*, August 1992.
8. Ephesians 6:4
9. Hebrews 11:25
10. Nicholas Davidson, "Life Without Father: An American Tragedy," *Policy Review* (Winter 1990). This is the quarterly publication of the Heritage Foundation, Washington, D.C.
11. Frank Trejo, "Striking a Balance," *Dallas Morning News*, 16 June 1989.
12. Hebrews 11:17
13. John 15:13
14. John 3:16
15. James C. Dobson, *Love Must Be Tough* (Waco, TX: Word, 1983), p. 44.
16. Jeremiah 6:14 TLB
17. Proverbs 17:6 TLB
18. *Los Angeles Times*, 6 August 1992, Associated Press news story.
19. Lindsey Tanner, "Teenage Mothers' History of Abuse," *Chicago Tribune*, 5 June 1990.
20. Mona Charen, "The Father's Role Is Vital to a Well-Knit Family," *Orange County Register*, 11 February 1992.
21. Davidson, "Life Without Father."
22. Children of the Night, a social service in Hollywood, CA.
23. John 15:26; 14:26
24. Psalm 3:3

Chapter 12
1. Leon J. Wood, *The Prophets of Israel* (Grand Rapids, MI: Baker Book House, 1979).
2. Isaiah 41:15
3. 2 Timothy 3:1
4. Jeremiah 51:30
5. 2 Peter 3:5-7 TLB
6. Revelation 21; 15:2
7. Luke 23:31
8. Romans 2:5-9
9. Romans 2:2
10. Romans 2:5
11. Romans 2:6
12. Romans 2:11
13. Romans 2:13
14. Romans 2:16
15. Romans 2:29, brackets added
16. Hebrews 4:12
17. See the book of Hosea.
18. 2 Corinthians 3:17
19. John 18:35
20. John 18:36
21. 1 Peter 2:9
22. Mark 16:15
23. Zechariah 4:10
24. 2 Thessalonians 2:11
25. 2 Thessalonians 2:3-4, 9-10

Chapter 13
1. Luke 19:45-46

MAJORING IN MEN®

A man that becomes a "real man" will influence his entire family to become faithful members of a local church in more than 90 percent of families. For more than 30 years, MAJORING IN MEN® training has equipped men to become "real." Nearly two million men in more than 100 nations and 80 languages have become "maximized" in their manhood through this simple yet effective outreach to men.

Start MAJORING IN MEN® curriculum and join one of the largest networks of men in the world with:

- Results-oriented training
- A time-tested track record
- Step-by-step process of success for lay leaders
- A global network of ministry resources
- Local church growth through multiplication of men

Join men around the world who are using MAJORING IN MEN® curriculum!

Pastor Michael Murphy, Sydney: "By far the best, most practical and powerful teaching series for men in the world today. We can plant more churches if we'll disciple more men!"

Pastor Joel Brooks, Michigan: "This curriculum will help any church raise faithful men. It's the reason I'm in ministry today!"

Start by studying a Leadership Kit, or the "MAXTrak" books and workbooks or get one of each book Dr. Cole wrote for your library. Whatever you do, start TODAY!

www.MAJORINGINMEN.com

CHRISTIAN MEN'S NETWORK

For more than 30 years, the ministry of Edwin Louis Cole, Christian Men's Network, has fought the battle for men. To host a men's event in your area or at your church, to launch MAJORING IN MEN® training in your area or at your church or to receive additional information about men's ministry, you may contact Christian Men's Network.

www.CMNWorld.com